ONE DAY AT A TIME

A VIETNAM DIARY

D.J. DENNIS

University of Queensland Press

First published 1992 by University of Queensland Press
Box 42, St Lucia, Queensland 4067 Australia

© D.J. Dennis 1992

This book is copyright. Apart from any fair dealing
for the purposes of private study, research, criticism
or review, as permitted under the Copyright Act, no
part may be reproduced by any process without written
permission. Enquiries should be made to the publisher.

Typeset by University of Queensland Press
Printed in Australia by The Book Printer, Victoria

Distributed in the USA and Canada by
International Specialized Book Services, Inc.,
5602 N.E. Hassalo Street, Portland, Oregon 97213-3640

Cataloguing in Publication Data
National Library of Australia

Dennis, D.J. (Donald James), 1945 .
   One day at a time: a Vietnam diary.

    1. Dennis, D.J. (Donald James), 1945- — Diaries.
    2. Vietnamese Conflict, 1961-1975 — Aerial operations, Australian.
    3. Tet Offensive, 1968 — Personal narratives, Australian. I. Title.

959.704348

ISBN 0 7022 2442 1

This book is dedicated to George Constable and Johnnie Fraser
— two mates who didn't make the Welcome Home Parade —
and to all Australian *grunts*, those indefatigable foot soldiers
whose skill and courage kept me safe during
that unforgettable year.

Acknowledgments

"In war the first casualty is truth."

During my year in Vietnam I kept a rough diary. Since then I've added to it whenever someone told me a story that dovetailed with the information I'd gathered. I soon discovered that what I remembered of an incident often differed from the way others recalled it. Sometimes the differences were minor; sometimes others gave those events an entirely new perspective. I found, too, that official records occasionally ignored or sanitised the same events. In some cases this is understandable; the task of recording every minute of every day of a ten-year involvement is impossible. However, the bureaucracy has an Orwellian predilection for rearranging facts or else contracting selective amnesia to conform with the politically sanctioned line of the day. And there are some skeletons in the closet which our military system prefers to keep locked away.

Even now, almost a quarter of a century later, old friends will frequently shed new light on an incident. Often a comparison with what *they* were doing at a certain time turns out to be outrageously comical — or tragic. To me, this highlights the fact that the Vietnam War was one of contrasts: while an Australian infantry company was in contact with the VC in the Long Hai Hills, other Aussie soldiers were chasing bar girls through the corridors of Vung Tau's notorious Grande Hotel. And while Vietnamese peasants were starving, the Saigon brass were dining on turkey and quaffing imported French champagne.

My problem was how to explain these contrasts without the narrative deteriorating into a hybrid of a *MASH* re-run and a *Rambo* script. Finally, after talking with old Army mates at the Welcome Home Parade in October 1987, I believed I'd found a way. The result, *One Day at a Time*, is an encapsulation of a single day in the Vietnam War from the viewpoints of several Australians.

The story is centred around the Army's 161 Reconnaissance Flight. Flying tiny unarmed Sioux helicopters and Cessna 180 aircraft, this small aviation unit was responsible for reconnaissance around the Task Force's operational area. I have set the narrative during February 1968, shortly after the start of the TET offensive: a particularly hectic period for the Australian Task Force.

This story is *not* an official history; rather, it's an anecdotal compilation of events guided by my diary, old friends and a sometimes flagging memory. Some of the incidents mentioned occurred at times other than those given; they are, however, based on fact and told, where possible, using the words of those involved — with minimal editing. Some names have been changed out of respect for those involved or their families. As far as I know, for example, there was no Sergeant Gavin Bucknell in the Third Battalion — however, there *was* an Australian soldier to whom the events described can be attributed.

Many former 161 Recce Flight members helped me with *One Day at a Time*. Ever willing to assist, they put up with my phone calls at odd hours, digging into memories and log books to find dates, names and locations. Among them: Paul Lipscombe (now Brigadier retired) who, as a junior Major, was the first officer to command 161 Recce Flight in Vietnam; Owen Eather, former Task Force Logistics officer and adopted 161 member (due to his ability to supply prime American beef); Paul "Paddy" O'Brien, 161 Flight's Rotary Wing section commander 1967-8 and (to my knowledge) the only Australian soldier to take his wife to Vietnam; Roger Colclough, who now flies helicopters for a charter company in Western Australia and lives as far away from the Army as he can without treading water; Ross Hutchinson, with whom I shared a tent for six months and whose snoring was worse than mine; Lt Colonel (retired) Glen Duus, a man who really knows the meaning of the word *premature* and still insists the Bin Gia SNAFU wasn't his fault; and Bernie "Father" Forrest, 161's Fixed Wing section commander, a master of the Cessna 180. He was always scheming ways of bombing General Westmoreland's Saigon HQ, but unfortunately never quite got round to it.

Steve Tizzard and Don Moffat rate special mention: Steve, for his ability to make the Cessna perform an Immelmann and reach near-sonic speed whenever ground fire was around; Don, for getting lost in a rain squall while returning from a last light recce then blundering into .50 cal fire from our own troops with me aboard . . . *during my last day in Vietnam*.

My gratitude to Andra Dahl and Barbara Ker Wilson for having faith, and my thanks to Dennis Smith and his group, whose assistance in editing sections of the first draft was invaluable.

I'm indebted to my wife Julie for putting up with the minor dramas that accompanied the writing of *One Day at a Time*. It musn't have been easy to live with constant reruns of the TET offensive.

D.J. Dennis
February 1992

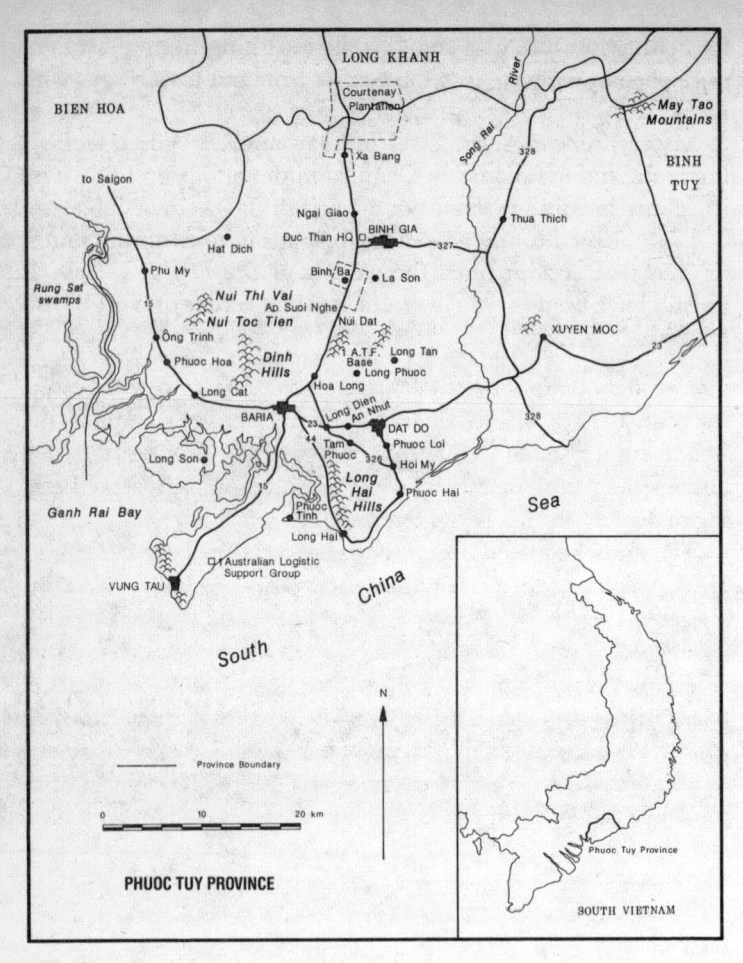

Map of Phuoc Tuy Province (from *Australians at War, Vietnam: The Australian Experience*. Courtesy Time-Life Books (Australia) Pty Ltd.)

VIETNAM, FEBRUARY 1968. THE AUSTRALIAN TASK FORCE BASE, NUI DAT

James Kelly was an advertising copywriter prior to his call up in 1966. After six months officer training he graduated as a Second Lieutenant. He was later posted to the Army's fledgling aviation unit in Vietnam. In typical Australian fashion he was nicknamed "Ned" by his mates.

James "Ned" Kelly

The artillery battery south of the airfield cracked six rounds over my tent. I snapped awake and lay on my bunk, listening to the freight-train rumble of 105mm shells as they flew out into the jungle. They exploded with hollow rolling thumps, like the beating of distant drums. I wondered who was dying.

The guns had been firing all night into suspected VC areas. Harassment and Interdiction fire — H and I — they called it, intended to keep the Viet Cong off their stroke and, one would have thought, us awake. But, as I'd discovered within a few days of arriving in Vietnam, the pounding of artillery became as much a part of the background noise as the clatter of helicopters. The sounds of war blended into a rumbling symphony that only drew one's attention if a discordant note was struck. Last night's fire mission sounded as if someone had stumbled in the percussion section. I'd slept fitfully.

I'd been dreaming of home, about the girls I knew. They seemed a world and a hundred years away. Yet it was only eighteen months since the Army had pointed its finger at me. Another six months and I could rejoin the real world. Take up where I'd left off. Maybe.

The TET offensive had come as a rude disruption to what had been for me an easy tour. It had taken considerable skill to wheedle my way out of being sent to one of the infantry battalions and into 161 Reconnaissance Flight. 161 was a small unit of about a hundred men. Its job, as the name suggested, was mainly reconnaissance. Our aircraft were small Cessna fixed-wing and Bell Sioux helicopters. They patrolled day and night, pilots and observers looking for signs indicating what the VC were up to. Flying at tree-top level, it was tedious, dangerous work, made even more hazardous by our lack of equipment and weapons.

I figured mine was probably one of the best jobs going — for a war. As operations officer it was my responsibility to oversee all aircraft sorties, schedule new ones and keep track of their whereabouts. It was mainly hours of routine interrupted by moments of panic or frustration. To relieve the tedium I could fly as observer whenever I wished — it definitely beat walking, something I was eager to avoid in a country littered with land-mines and booby traps.

Apart from the fact that I was a reluctant conscript, I just wasn't cut out to be a grunt. Despite constant ridicule from the other services, grunts are very special people. Even the epithet *grunt* (meant to convey the exertion of soldiering) was said with affection in the Australian Army. They are tough buggers, able to withstand extreme privation, pain and terror yet still come up smiling. But I figured I'd had my share of running around the bush, crawling through mud, receiving barbed wire cuts, grazed shins and sore feet during training.

However, I still experienced twinges of conscience every time the grunts left Nui Dat on operations. I'd watch the lines of Hueys clatter in, pick up their loads then flutter away. When they returned a week or two later, I'd stand on the road beside the airfield, keeping an eye out for friends I'd gone to school with or mates I'd made during training. All too often the count was short. It was hard to take, especially when the majority of Australians back home didn't give a damn.

Despite these reservations, I vowed to stay in one piece. To hell with the glory. The thought of creeping through the jungle terrified me. I was too big, I hated the heat and I could barely run to save my life — and with my size fourteen boots, I figured I'd be unlucky enough to tread on two mines simultaneously. The last thing I aspired to was being a legless hero. They could keep their medals, I was content to remain safe behind the wire, venturing out in our aircraft for a bird's eye view of the war to satisfy any sudden macho impulses. The VC weren't going to get this little brown duck, no, sir.

I buried my face in my pillow, tried to recapture my dream,

but the guns cracked again and scattered the images. Once more the sound of drums, this time a little closer. At least it was outgoing.

I rolled on my back and peered up through the gap between the tent's sandbagged wall and its canvas roof. Silhouettes of rubber trees were emerging against the sky. The air was tinged with a coolness that would be burned away when the sun exploded above the horizon. It was the dry season and it was going to be hot. But then it was always hot in Vietnam.

I glanced at my watch: 0530 hrs. Another thirty minutes and I was due on duty in the Flight's command post. Today we had a busy schedule. Two of the Task Force's three infantry battalions and much of our supporting armour and artillery had been sent to help the Americans defend the Ben Hoa airbase, some thirty kilometres west. Half of 161 Flight's aircraft had gone with this battle group, leaving us only three helicopters and two fixed-wing to cover the Province. This created an extra workload as we were flying reconnaissance patrols around the clock looking for signs of an enemy build-up in our area. With Nui Dat's defences thin on the ground, those of us remaining were growing apprehensive about an attack on the base. And it wasn't only the TET offensive that had interrupted my cosy sinecure — people in high places seemed determined to cause me even more grief.

Although we were an independent unit, our orders came from Task Force HQ. Bullshit Castle, as it was called by the less reverent, was tucked away in the centre of the base, about a kilometre away, and linked to our CP by phone and radio. The Staff officer there responsible for coordinating air operations was known by his appointment title of Seagull (Air). When I'd first arrived, Seagull was a senior major who, while demanding a high level of performance, had been easy to work with. We'd got on well and operations between our command post and Task Force HQ had proceeded with only minor drama.

Unfortunately, a month ago the Major had been shipped home after being wounded in a mortar attack. He was temporarily replaced by an ambitious captain who'd previously filled an obscure posting on Task Force HQ. For him the position was his big chance for stardom. Rumour had it he was determined to prove himself in the job and gain early promotion. A book-man who was always searching for flaws in others so he could brown-nose to the Senior Staff, I promptly dubbed the little turd "Captain Queeg", after the paranoid ship's captain in *The Caine Mutiny*. Our Queeg even looked like Humphrey Bogart. With cropped black hair and a pug face, all he needed was a handful of clicking steel balls to complete the image.

Queeg's demands were often impossible. 161 Flight had eight helicopters and four fixed-wing aircraft on strength; some days twice that number were needed to meet Task Force's requirements. He'd soon gauged my hot spot, promising that if I failed to cooperate one hundred percent he'd see me assigned to the Task Force reinforcement unit. That really spooked me: the reinforcement unit was a pool of surplus personnel used to replace battle casualties. They made themselves useful by patrolling the jungle around Nui Dat.

So I cooperated. But I was nearing the end of my tether, I could be pushed just so far. I hadn't asked to become involved in this war and if need be I'd turn peacenik, fairy — anything to avoid stepping foot outside the base. Although I didn't realise it at the time, Queeg had become the focus of my frustrations with being a small cog in a giant, impersonal machine that seemed incapable of being stopped or even steered in the right direction.

Fortunately, the only contact I had with Queeg was via the phone or when I went to Task Force HQ for the afternoon briefing. Recently, though, as enemy activity around the Province increased, Queeg had been on the phone to our Command Post almost hourly. He wanted updates of our aircrafts' locations, serviceability states, pilot strengths, reams of statistics that kept his staff busy sticking pins in a huge wall map. I got the distinct impression that he was bent on creating an empire for himself. His predecessor had been content with a modest cubby hole in Task Force HQ, but Queeg had gone on the expansion trail and within a week his operations room resembled a Battle of Britain command centre. Only the WAAFs were missing, pushing little airplane models around a plot table.

I wondered what today's activity would bring. No doubt Queeg would be looking for any opportunity to win Brownie points at my expense, so I resolved to be two steps ahead of him. The problem was, with our Commanding Officer away the flight's detachment to Ben Hoa, Queeg regarded himself as my *de facto* commander. I figured he was trying to expand his empire and I vowed to be as uncooperative with him as I could manage without reaching the point of blatant insubordination. With luck I could score a few points of my own.

I reached for the lamp on the ammunition crate beside my bed and flicked it on. Its yellow light shone in a puddle around my corner of the tent. Opposite, I could hear John Devlin snoring softly. He'd been flying until early morning, trying to locate NVA units the Task Force Intelligence people believed were now moving into the Province. I'd flown as his observer on one sortie, using our only night vision device, a starscope I'd "acquired" from the Americans. We'd found nothing.

Reluctantly I swung my feet to the floor, leaned forward and squinted at the calendar pinned to the wall. I picked up a pencil and struck off another day, realising with intense pleasure that this was day 182 — I *only* had 183 to go. One more and I'd be on the downhill run. Then I'd board the Qantas Freedom Bird at Saigon airport and relax in air-conditioned comfort as the big jet whisked me back to the real world. There'd be no more pounding guns, no more clattering helicopters, and no more living each day wondering when the VC were going to hit us. There'd also be no more Queeg to give me heat every hour on the hour.

I glanced at John, suddenly filled with envy. He was a short-timer with only fifteen days to go. Counting days was an obsession with all of us. Almost everyone knew exactly how many remained before they were due to return home. The lesser the days, the greater one's status. New arrivals rated lowest. With three hundred and sixty-five days to go they were regarded as shmucks who believed they were going to make a significant contribution to winning the war. They soon learned otherwise.

As I stood and groped for my shaving gear, the guns fired again. Another six rounds thundered off to blast some remote patch of jungle into submission. This time the drumbeat of exploding shells announced the start of another day.

Good Morning, Vietnam.

Second Lieutenant Mike Dawson was a national serviceman who'd volunteered to be trained as an Army pilot. Prior to the draft he'd worked in a bank. Now, after two years of training, he found himself on his way to Vietnam.

My first glimpse of Vietnam was as a passenger in a Qantas Boeing 707. That's the way the Australian Army delivered me to war, in a chartered jet complete with Muzak and free booze. As I peered out of the window I almost expected to see armies clashing on the rice fields below, while artillery and napalm blasted the surrounding jungle.

I'm sure this simplistic image was inspired by the media coverage the war was receiving back home. When the TET offensive broke out, hardly an evening went by without a report from some steely-eyed journalist who seemed to be where the fighting was the bloodiest. (Later I found out that many "action" reports were stage-managed by journalists or cameramen in base areas.) According to the press the Americans were badly shaken by the mass attacks and were now regaining the ground they'd lost.

As we descended I felt a surge of anxiety. So far it had all been part of a big game: the training, lectures and combat familiarisation, all frighteningly efficient and a touch Gung Ho. It was over two years since I'd walked into the recruiting depot with a thousand other conscripts. During basic training I'd chosen Army Aviation. Although this meant signing on for five years to repay the cost of training, I'd figured that with luck, Vietnam would be over before I'd finished flight school. I would then serve out the remainder of my time chalking up hours in Australia and walk into a job with one of the domestic airlines. I'd miscalculated badly.

This was the day I never thought would come. Even a few weeks before I was due to depart, we'd been assured the Americans had a positive grip on the situation. There'd been talk from General Westmoreland about seeing light at the end of the Vietnam tunnel — soon it would all be over. Unfortunately, his glimmer of hope turned out to be an express train called the TET offensive. The day after the offensive broke out, Westmoreland appeared on evening television with a wide-eyed expression that looked as if he'd been mounted by a herd of bull elephants. He told us that TET was all dirty pool on the enemy's part, but not to worry, everything was again in hand. America would prevail. Sadly, I realised, here was a commander who'd lost the plot, with no firm grip at all on the situation.

Suddenly the war was no longer an abstract sand model exercise in some distant never-to-be-reached time-frame. It was *now*. From the air, however, Vietnam looked deceptively peaceful. A green patchwork quilt cut by the silver-gold fingers of the Mekong Delta was emerging from the darkness like a developing Polaroid. Instead of a ravaged, burning landscape, it looked like a page from a tourist brochure. I was disappointed. I believed a war should look like one of those huge cracked brown paintings of Waterloo which portrayed a mountain of tangled humanity storming some distant goal. Like many of my generation, most of my impressions of war had been influenced by the Anzac legend and over-exposure to *Henry V* while in high school. Even the nightly television coverage had failed to dispel totally that naive imagery.

The seatbelt sign winked on, snapping me from my reverie. As the cabin crew prepared for landing, I noticed they were avoiding us, minimising conversation and eye contact. After we left Sydney they'd been full of talk as they treated us like any plane-load of tourists. But this all-male crew, taken on during a four hour stopover in Manila, had remained distant, almost sullen. It was as if they'd been instructed not to fraternise with us for fear of catching some terrible disease. I now know they realised that some of us would be making the flight home in the cargo hold. It's difficult to be chatty under those circumstances.

The Boeing dropped through a thin layer of pink cloud and emerged into bright sunshine. Light shafted through the windows and painted little square haloes along the cabin above some of the soldier's heads. I wondered if it was a final benediction to an unfortunate few.

On the ground I see villages scattered amongst the fields, roads crammed with vehicles and tiny people-specks. The aircraft banks steeply onto final approach. We whistle over sprawling slums surrounding Saigon. Kids are playing in the gutters.

Others are swimming in a water-filled bomb crater near a shattered house. No one looks up. They go about their lives as if it's normal for jets to fly low up the main street. Later I learned it was.

We rumble over a rice paddy surrounding the airfield. I see a famer plodding knee-deep in mud behind a water buffalo. He looks up. I glimpse a wrinkled brown face beneath a conical straw hat. He holds out a claw-like hand and gives us the finger.

Welcome to Vietnam

"161 Reconnaissance Flight's radio callsigns will be known as POSSUM."

Standard Operating Procedures

NUI DAT

Ned Kelly

The eastern sky was shading pink as I trudged the leafy track through the rubber trees to a corrugated iron shed that served as our showers. The plumbing consisted of four canvas buckets slung from a roof beam. I filled one with tepid water from a storage tank, hauled it up and scrubbed myself. Before it emptied, I quickly shaved. I then dried off, wrapped a towel around my midriff and headed back to my tent, avoiding my morning constitutional. The war was no respecter of human dignity in the most unexpected ways. Sitting on one of the seats in our four-poster field dunny was hazardous when the artillery was firing overhead. The shells created a shock wave which compressed the air in the septic pit with enough force to lift the weighted lids on each stand. If you were caught, the sudden pressure made your eyes bulge and ears pop. So, as the guns cracked again, I gave the little green shed a wide berth.

The plantation was a mosaic of vertical lines and shafting sunlight. Beneath the trees our tents crouched in long rows, their dusty canvas and high sandbagged walls giving them a sad permanence that denied any hope the war's end was near. The air was warm. Insects buzzed. Somewhere far away our diesel generator throbbed at its endless task. From the tents around me transistor radios tuned to Armed Forces Radio created an eerie stereophonic effect. *"We're Sergeant Pepper's Lonely Heart's Club Band, we hope you will enjoy the show . . ."* The music cut the morning silence like fingernails on a blackboard.

In peace time, rubber tappers would already be at work in this plantation. Their knife scars could still be seen on the tree trunks: V-shaped slashes across the bark, like stripes of rank. I wondered how much of the rubber produced here had found its way back home. Maybe I'd actually driven on tyres made from one of these trees. It was a possibility — most of the plantations were owned by rubber companies whose products were distributed worldwide and it was rumoured they paid the VC hefty bribes so they could continue production; Tyres were helping finance the bullets being fired at us. An odd thought for the day, I reflected.

The artillery banged another six rounds away. This time I noted they were firing into the Nui Thi Vis, a cluster of haze-shrouded hills about ten kilometres west that was home for a local VC unit. The salvo was a morning ritual, a wake-up call to remind the enemy we were ready for action if they wanted to take us on. Today, however, I likened it to poking a stick in a hornet's nest. The VC just might accept the challenge.

When I reached my tent, John Devlin was lying on his back staring at the canvas roof. "Fifteen days and a wake-up to go," he announced as I pulled on my boots.

"Lucky bastard," I swore, envious of the state of grace he'd achieved. Short timers, particularly those with less than thirty days left, were regarded with reverence. I wondered if I should genuflect before speaking to him in future.

"Two weeks and I'll be in the land of the vertical pussy," John leered.

I hurled my boot at him. It collapsed his mosquito net then bounced onto the floor. I snatched it up and scurried from the tent before John could untangle himself.

The sun was chasing the last shadows as I hoped the short distance to the officers' mess, an open-sided tin hut with a flywire enclosure at one end. We speculated that even the insects in Vietnam were VC and the wire was essential to delay them long enough for us to eat before they broke through and snatched the food from our plates. Breakfast for me was two slabs of toast and a cup of coffee. Because I was always up before the regular breakfast serving time I made my own. We had a big toaster that I'd load with bread, then imagine I was back home as I savoured the aroma. The ritual took about ten minutes. That morning I toasted three thick slabs — for some reason our cook's bread had been tasting better lately. It had a mild spicy flavour we attributed to his experimenting with local recipes.

Clutching my toast and coffee, I headed for the flight's command post. The artillery cracked again. This time the rounds flew north. Our gunners were really putting Charley on notice this morning. Obviously something was about to happen.

We are Fighting for Peace! Sign near the entrance to the 91st TAC Fighter Wing, Tan Son Nhut Airbase, Saigon.

Fighting for a piece of what? — Scrawled beneath.

TAN SON NHUT AIRBASE, SAIGON. 0600HRS

Mike Dawson

". . . thank you for flying Qantas," the aircraft captain quipped as we shuffled down the aisle to the strains of *Blue Hawaii*. As I neared the door, the twang of ukeleles was smothered by the howl of jet engines. I stepped from the aircraft into another world. The heat hit me in a solid wave that took my breath. The sun was barely above the horizon, but already its fire reflected from the aircraft's wings, the tarmac and nearby buildings. My eyes ached. Going down the steps the handrails were warm. I reached the ground and felt the heat soak up through the soles of my boots. My first thought was: *God, how am I going to stand this climate for a year?* And the place stank; a sickly sweet aroma, like rotting fruit tinged with frangipanni. It was the smell of Asia.

Instead of a pretty girl placing a garland of flowers around our necks, we were met by a fat Australian Air Force Sergeant.

Clutching a clipboard between blunt fingers, he climbed awkwardly from a lopsided jeep, waddled over to us and announced that Caribou transports would soon arrive to fly us to Nui Dat and Vung Tau. We were split into groups of thirty and told to wait. The Sergeant glanced at his watch, muttered something about breakfast, then squeezed aboard his jeep and sped away towards a cluster of distant buildings.

Already a tanker was pumping fuel into the 707. The flight crew gathered in the shade beneath its wings, incongruous in their crisp civilian uniforms and with anxious looks on their faces. They knew they didn't belong here and were eager to get back to the real world. It was ironic that they'd earned more danger money for this one flight than we received for a year's combat pay.

Our duffles had been stacked on the tarmac. As we collected them about a hundred and fifty Australian soldiers filed past, all lean, mean and tanned. They were in high spirits and wore the ribbons of the Vietnam campaign on their chests. As they climbed the stairs into what a few minutes ago had been our aircraft, they rubbed in the fact that we had three hundred and sixty-five days to go. We suckers!

When it was put that way — a year sounds much shorter than three hundred and sixty-five days — I felt miserable. I tried to shake it off, but secretly wished it was all behind me and I was with the group now leaving. "Nobody has three hundred and sixty-five days to go," was an expression I would come to loathe in the next twenty-four hours.

I watched the Qantas 707 prepared for take-off. Smiling faces at windows, waves and lewd gestures. As the doors shut we all fell silent. The gates to the civilised world had been closed, the final avenue of escape barred. Even the faces at the windows seemed to share our emotions. Erect fingers gave way to hands pressed against perspex. I'll always remember one, straining white as if the owner was trying to retain contact with us . . . or a mate he'd left behind. For a moment there was a bond as our fears reached out and met their reassurances somewhere above the tarmac. Then the aircraft lurched forward and swung around in a shimmering kerosene haze. It screeched away and disappeared behind the revetments, only its tail with the red kangaroo symbol visible.

We looked nervously at each other. We were the new kids on the block in the roughest part of town. How many of us would be making the flight home in three hundred and sixty-five days? Who would be going home in a box? We didn't want to know.

We caught sight of the aircraft as it climbed out and banked south. The sun flashed from its wings in a final salute, then it was gone. It would land in Sydney in eight hours.

I shut out thoughts of home and tried to come to terms with reality. I wanted to find the next aircraft and smuggle myself aboard, but my conscience wouldn't let me. How would it look if I returned home a quivering mound of jelly, without having heard a shot fired in anger? That would be no way for an heir to the ANZAC legend to behave. So, along with the others, who I sensed shared my fears, I quietly watched and tried not to dwell on my situation.

At that time Tan Son Nhut was the busiest airport in the world, with military traffic creating the biggest swarm of aircraft I'd ever seen. The airfield covered a vast area, stretching to the horizon where we could just see lines of shattered palm trees. Its bullet and shrapnel scarred civil terminals were now almost hidden by prefab military structures. There were revetments by the hundred, with aircraft of all sizes parked inside their protective blast walls. The runways were in continual use. From each, queues of arriving and departing aircraft streamed to both horizons. In the first five minutes I recognised almost every aircraft in the US inventory. The noise was overpowering. Underscoring the howl of jet engines was the throbbing rhythm of helicopters — the theme song of the war. To this day it still makes my stomach churn when I hear the echoing thump of approaching rotor blades.

Nearby, a USAF C-141 cargo jet was being loaded. We'd watched as the lumbering aircraft touched down, taxied to a halt, then disgorged hundreds of crisply uniformed American soldiers. They double-timed across the tarmac, chanting like a football cheer squad and snapped to a halt before a flag-draped reception committee. Drums rattled, bugles tooted; a glockenspiel added its incongruous tinkle to the cacophony around us. *"Be kind to your webbed footed friends . . ."*

A convoy of trucks wheeled onto the tarmac and the new arrivals were whisked away, leaving us wondering about the efficiency of the Australian transport system that left us to broil in the sun.

A few minutes later a tanker rolled up to the C-141 and began refuelling. After the tanker pulled away, two flatbed semis filled with palletised freight queued at the aircraft's cargo ramp. We looked on, noticing the pallets were stacked with slab-sided metal containers dripping with condensation. It made me want to reach out and run a hand along their flanks, to relive the smooth feel of a frosted beer can on a summer's day. It was a pleasant reminder that somewhere in this tropical sauna, cold still existed. The ground crew quickly started rolling the pallets into the hold.

What impressed us was the American's production line efficiency. They didn't waste a minute; soldiers were delivered, the aircraft refuelled, then ten pallets of cargo loaded in less time than took us to collect our baggage. It was reassuring to see such a well oiled military machine in action. At least the Yanks were organised.

Our admiration was short lived. As the aircraft's clamshell doors hissed shut, we realised that the cold metal containers were coffins.

NUI DAT. 0600HRS

Ned Kelly

Our flight command post occupied almost half of our administration centre — a long tin hut surrounded by a sandbagged blast wall. When I first arrived in Vietnam, the CP was a dim little room cluttered with radios and telephones, nothing like the nerve centres I'd admired in movies such as *The Dam Busters* or *Twelve O'Clock High*. I'd decided something more appropriate was needed. So in a series of lunchtime raids on the engineer's stores depot, I stole truckloads of material for its reconstruction.

During alterations, I expanded the wall dividing the area almost a metre. This required a midnight rebuild of the orderly room and the Second-in-Command's office. They had so much space they didn't notice the sudden contraction of their walls, although the 21C did comment the morning after: "I feel as if things are closing in on me." I hinted he was suffering battle fatigue and should take a few days R and R in Vang Tau. That he did; while he was getting his tubes cleared I carved another foot off his office.

Our command post now looked the part. Its walls were covered with maps, a flight schedule board and *Playboy* centrefolds. A long bench crammed with radios and field telephones filled one end of the room. Three rows of folding canvas chairs faced a large map of the Province. But still there were none of those WAAFS with long sticks, pushing little airplane models around a plot table.

One touch I'd added was a bulky World War Two microphone rescued from a junk pile at a US base. I'd scrubbed the chrome-plate to its original art-deco glory and put it in a place of honour on the bench among the radios. Beneath it was a sign: SPEAK TO THE PILOTS — ONLY 100 PIASTRES. By picking it up and screaming obscenities, it served as a means of letting off steam. It was used regularly.

Since the outbreak of the TET offensive we'd been expecting the VC to attack Nui Dat. So every night we'd been on stand-to readiness with the base blacked out. Although we knew the enemy was well aware of our location, we weren't about to make it easier by providing them with aiming points for their rockets and mortars. It was how I imagined the London blitz would have been, with everyone on the lookout for giveaway chinks of light.

For almost a month we'd kept up this routine. The CP's dimmed lighting and black hessian curtains gave it a conspiratorial atmosphere, full of whispering shadows like the secret lairs haunted by Nazis in old B grade movies. However, instead of a portrait of Adolph gazing sternly down from the wall, our Fuhrer was a pouting Miss September with her knees draped over her ears and a belly full of staples.

During the past week, however, the urgency of the alert had eased. The base remained untouched, almost as if the VC were avoiding us. The blackout had been reduced to a brownout, and after the one hundred per cent stand-to at sundown, limited activity resumed. Beer was on sale in the soldiers' canteen again and the evening movie was screened. A new, poker-faced film star named Eastwood was suddenly the rage, killing more bad guys each night than the Task Force chalked up in a month. For us, the TET offensive was being upstaged by spaghetti westerns.

The duty officer last night had been Lieutenant Ross Hutchinson. When I arrived at the CP, Hutch gave me a quick briefing. The only action of immediate concern was a VC attack during the night on Xuyen Moc village, about twenty clicks east of Nui Dat. Xuyen Moc was defended by a small ARVN (Army of the Republic of Vietnam) unit, helped by an Australian two-man advisory team. They'd fought off the VC but had taken heavy casualties and our standby helicopter might be needed later in the morning to fly in medical supplies. Task Force would advise us as soon as they'd clarified the situation. There was nothing else except the usual series of suspected enemy sightings around the Province. Hutch headed for the showers. I pulled the curtains and let the day stream in.

I checked the Intelligence reports from MACV (Military Assistance Command Vietnam — General Westmoreland's HQ). There was more action around Saigon, while Hue and Khe San were still under siege. The Yanks were shooting anything that moved and bombing most things that didn't. Meanwhile Westmoreland was asking congress for another two hundred thousand troops to "stabilise" the situation.

Westmoreland was a worry. I know it's the done thing for soldiers to knock senior officers, but I'd seen him when he'd inspected the Task Force a few months ago. From a distance he looked every bit the definitive American general: tall, flinty-eyed, square-jawed. But up close he wasn't so tall and his eyes were vacant orbs hiding beneath giant, hairy brows which gave me the distinct impression that while his lights were on no one was at home. From then on I was grateful our commanders had decided we would operate independently of the Americans.

The daily action reports being churned out by Westmoreland's staff only added to my fears. His HQ had been raided by a VC commando team during the opening hours of the

TET offensive and now his staff were determined to hide the fact that Westy had been caught with his pants down. MACV listed thousands of enemy dead, most of which we regarded as suspect. A typical anecdote told how a US Army battalion commander had inflated his body count after an artillery bombardment shredded a lone VC:

"Here's a head, that's one VC dead. There's a leg, that's two, and, goddamn it, here's another leg — that's three. Look there's an arm. That makes four enemy killed. Well done soldier, have a Silver Star!"

Obviously MACV's action reports were being written by conscripted pulp novelists keeping their hand in before returning to Hollywood. I decided Westmoreland wouldn't have known if his arse was ablaze until the fire brigade filled his trousers with water. Trouble was, he was determined to fight this war to the last man, and that included us.

To add to my scepticism there was an alarming report from our Task Force HQ. Intelligence had information indicating that a large North Vietnamese Force was heading our way. The NVA's aim was to wipe out the Task Force.

I'd heard it all before. Radio Hanoi's broadcasts were regularly promising us Imperialist Lackeys that we'd be slaughtered to the last man unless we surrendered — or better still, defected to Hanoi to receive a plot of communal paddyfield and a night in the cot with a sloe-eyed maiden as a reward. None of us wanted to spend the rest of our lives as expatriate rice farmers, and the only near-takers were those perpetually randy Aussies to whom the free sex sounded attractive. But even they soon calculated it was easier to spend ten bucks for a blow job in a Vung Tau steam-and-cream parlor than trudge the thousand or so kilometres up the bomb-peppered Ho Chi Min trail to North Vietnam.

So the "Alamo Scenario", as the constant threat of annihilation became known, was always taken with a grain of salt. However, this morning Task Force Int's story struck a nerve. Then I realised — it was basically a rework of the recon information we'd been feeding *them*. Even so, coming from higher authority and printed in crisp military jargon, it looked infinitely more credible. I wished we hadn't been so diligent. Sometimes it's better not to know.

As the artillery banged out another sonata, Sergeant Dave Brown walked into the CP. He was a tall beanstalk of a man who chattered at high speed like a TV commercial.

"Morning, sir. Looks like another fine day," he greeted me cheerily. He slung his rifle in the rack then went to a wall calendar and struck off another day. Keeping track of everyone's time in country was Brown's hobby. He scratched in a new name, stood back and grinned. "Lieutenant Dawson's arriving today. Poor bugger. No bastard's got three hundred and sixty-five days to go."

I glanced at the calendar. He'd also crossed off another day for me. One eighty-three to go. I savoured the moment again. It was all downhill from tomorrow.

"What's new?" Brown asked.

I tossed him the Task Force Intelligence report. "Those whackers over at Int are at it again. They suspect *another* NVA regiment is headed our way."

Brown flipped through the document. "Is that the one we found north-east of here?" He peered at the map; "or the one Task Force reckon *they* found north-east of here?"

"The one they claim *they* found *is* the one *we* found," I replied. Our aircraft had sighted an enemy base camp area under construction in heavy jungle four months ago and we'd been watching it ever since. The report had been going round in circles, growing every time it passed through the Task Force hierarchy.

Brown nodded sagely. "Could be something to it this time. The VC haven't tried anything against this place for ages. It's about time they took a poke at us."

I frowned. "Damn it! Task Force's been preaching that line for the last three weeks. They think it's their job to frighten us with stories like this to keep us on our toes. They're full of bullshit!"

Brown windmilled a long arm at the map. "Maybe so, but everyone else in Vietnam has been hit hard. We've got off lightly so far. Maybe our time has come."

Like many soldiers I'd become superstitious, believing if you talked bad news long enough it became reality. But I knew Dave was right. It was months since we'd received even a token mortaring from the VC. Meanwhile, American bases were being splattered with high explosives daily.

"Perhaps we don't rate the VC's attention," I suggested hopefully. I was tired of attack alerts and their associated drama. All I wanted to do was get out of the place. The VC could over-run Nui Dat after I'd left. Maybe I could fake a bout of insanity . . .

"Could be. But the longer they leave it, the bigger the attack will be when it comes." Brown put the clipboard on its hook then settled in a chair behind the bench. He tuned his transistor radio to the American Armed Forces station, AFVN. The time signal beeped the hour and the disk jockey screamed his introduction. *"Good Morning, Vee-et-nam!"*

From our tent lines, the cookhouse, the latrines — from all around the Task Force a soldier chorus echoed like the response to a Mezzuin's cry: *"Fuck Vee-et-nam!"*

Situation normal. I knew the day they screamed they loved Vietnam we'd be in big trouble.

"The peasants are restless," Brown muttered. He was one of those philosophical types who read deep meaning into everything — not at all like the average, rather pragmatic senior NCO. At first he'd been hard to take, but after a few weeks I'd grown to like the old fart (he was thirty-two). More importantly he'd accepted me, a shiny new second lieutenant, as his leader. At least that's what I thought.

"The coms checks," I ordered as I reached for the nearest PRC-25 radio. We had four radios, plus field telephones linking us to Task Force HQ and our tiny one-man control tower atop Nui Dat hill. It was possible to reach Vang Tau with one of the phones, and from there, occasionally, the outside world. That phone had been painted red and a sign reminded users Charlie was listening. (The VC left the lines intact, figuring by doing so they could listen in.)

We made the checks, including picking up the red phone and saying, "Good morning, Charley," to an eavesdropping

Vietcong agent we assumed was up a palm tree somewhere between Nui Dat and Vung Tau.

Every morning started with the first light recons. They were flights out to and around what was known as lines Alpha and Bravo; Alpha being the maximum range of enemy mortar fire, about five thousand metres, and Bravo the limits of the Task Force's own field artillery, around twelve thousand metres. It was a sound precaution, the theory being if the VC was preparing for a dawn attack we'd be able to spot them or their supporting artillery. The infantry constantly had patrols covering the same areas, ambushing tracks, river crossings, any place the VC might pass through during the night. After first light the patrols would move on, continually sweeping the areas, making it difficult for the VC to approach Nui Dat in force without being discovered.

This combination of infantry patrols and aerial reconnaissance kept Nui Dat a relatively safe place to live. I was eager for it to stay that way. This morning we had one helicopter and one fixed-wing assigned to the first light recon. After covering the mandatory lines Alpha and Bravo areas they were tasked to concentrate on the north-west and north-east sectors. These areas had been a hive of activity for months now and a source of frustration to us all. Every morning the first light recon had reported signs of overnight enemy activity: keel marks and footprints on the beach where sampans had come ashore, even ox-carts on the highways miles from the nearest village, obviously returning from a night of hauling VC supplies. But day after day, Task Force HQ accepted our reports and we saw little reaction to them.

One fixed-wing pilot, Steve Tizzard, totally pissed off by HQ's apparent lack of interest, had even gone as far as submitting his recon report tagged with a suggestion that the senior staff should consider installing traffic lights on a highway junction near the ruins of a village to the north-east called Thua Tich. Such was the volume of VC ox-cart traffic, Steve suggested, that "the VC run extraordinary risks of coming to grief in traffic accidents". Task Force's reaction was to award Steve a week as duty officer.

We knew our recons contributed to the overall picture of enemy activity and that it was unrealistic to expect Task Force HQ to react instantly to everything we found. But for once we'd like to see HQ do something — anything — to convince us our efforts weren't being wasted.

As the first helicopter spluttered into life on the flight line, I expected today would be much like the rest. We'd find the enemy and the report would be filed on a giant spike somewhere in the bowels of Task Force HQ along with all the rest of the bumpf sent by other units.

Peter ("Pedro") Taylor was piloting the chopper. He came up on our flight net for a quick radio check, then lifted from the pad. As he climbed away I marked the flight task board with his time-out, then sat down and sipped my coffee. I knew Pedro wasn't heading for lines Alpha or Bravo. This morning he was heading straight for the beach.

Pedro Taylor

I wasn't carrying an observer that morning, I'd decided to fly the first light recon alone. I didn't want any witnesses to see what I was about to do. I lifted off and headed directly into the sunrise. The sky was pink, incredibly beautiful, with tiny wisps of mist clinging to the trees like cotton wool. The sun hadn't yet thinned the air and the engine was developing full power. With only myself on board, the old bird felt unusually sprightly, and as the shadows lifted from the ground I dropped to tree-top level and enjoyed the ride. I was heading for the coast due east of Nui Dat. There the beaches were long strips of white sand not unlike those on the east coast of Australia. But I wasn't going there to look at the waves.

Three days ago one of our fixed-wing aircraft had spotted an old man sitting on the beach about thirty clicks up the coast from the village of Phuoc Hai. I'd been on recon in the area and our CP asked me to divert and check him out. Ned Kelly was my observer that day and when we reached the coast we saw the old man standing by the water's edge, waves tugging at his bare feet.

We were flying about ten feet above the sand and as we approached I expected him to bolt inland. But he just stood and calmly watched us.

I circled him cautiously. He was thin, with hunched shoulders and a sad, wrinkled face framed by a scraggly beard and silver hair. He wore a torn white shirt with tattered brown trousers rolled up to his bony knees. He wasn't carrying any weapons and didn't look like an enemy soldier to me. All he needed was a fishing rod to complete the china-shop figurine image.

The old man raised a scrawny hand to shield his eyes from the sun, squinted up at us, then returned his attention to the sea. Ned looked across at me, shook his head, and applied the safety on the M-60 resting across his knees. The old man wasn't enemy.

I climbed to a hundred feet and checked the area. He was on a stretch of sand about two hundred metres wide. Inland, the beach filtered into sparse jungle. This wasn't a likely site for an ambush, so I slowed to a near hover.

The old man turned his back on us disdainfully then plodded towards a pile of crates stacked above the waterline. They were wrapped in woven palm mats and tied with rope. Marks in the sand showed where they'd been dragged up the beach. He sat down on the crates and ignored us. Farther north I could see wooden planks and more crates scattered along the high tide mark. It looked as if a ship had been wrecked during the night and the crates were part of its cargo. Perhaps the old man was from its crew.

I radioed my finding to Task Force HQ and received a disinterested acknowledgment. I circled for ten minutes, then because I was low on fuel, decided there wasn't much point hanging around. I made one last circuit and as I turned towards Nui Dat, Ned gave the old guy a wave. I was damned if he didn't flash a quick smile and return the wave.

Back at Nui Dat I'd reported our findings. It was obvious the old man had been shipwrecked, Task Force agreed; they'd received reports about the crew of a trading junk wrecked in a storm, washing ashore farther south near Phuoc Hai. I suggested that a helicopter could be sent to pick up the old boy, as he was almost thirty kilometres from the nearest village. Task Force said they'd look into it.

That evening, one of our Cessnas on the last light recon reported the old man still sitting on his crates. Once again Task Force HQ was advised, and once again they said they'd look into sending a helicopter to pick him up. But they did nothing.

The following morning we sighted him again — it seemed he had no intention of moving. That day I flew the last light recon with Ned Kelly along as observer. Ned had been trying to convince Task Force that the old guy was harmless and had brought a polaroid camera with him to take photos to back his argument. Again we circled, Ned snapped some photos then waved, the old man waved back and we flew away. Despite the photos and our OC's intervention, Task Force HQ still did nothing.

We discussed picking him up ourselves but it was risky. The old man was slap in the middle of enemy territory and we could be walking into an ambush. What was needed was a light fire team to fly top cover while one chopper landed. If push came to shove, we figured we could do it ourselves using two Sioux, one carrying an observer with an M-60, the other to pick him up. A fixed-wing armed with rockets could fly top cover. It was cumbersome, but it would work. However, Task Force put an end to our plans by forbidding us to fly such a mission. So we left the old man on the beach.

During the following days, each time our aircraft flew past he was reported to be looking progressively worse for wear. Without a hat, his face had been blistered by the sun, and he was now painfully thin. He'd built a lean-to among his crates, using their palm mat wrapping, and I could see where he'd made a cooking fire. Near the waterline, where the sand was cut by tidal pools, he'd used bamboo and tree branches to build a fish trap. He'd settled in like a regular Robinson Crusoe, surrounded by squawking gulls, which he also caught and ate. Why he hadn't tried walking south to Phuoc Hai we could only guess — we assumed he didn't know the area.

After three days we gave up appealing to Task Force HQ. They were busy with the action around Ben Hoa and it was obvious that the old man was way down their list of priorities. So

Ned and I decided if we couldn't pick him up, at least we could help him walk to the nearest village.

We made up a survival kit. It included a bush hat, a large tube of burn cream, bandages, string, a pocket knife, even a hundred metres of fishing line with hooks and sinkers scrounged from one of our own survival kits. I cut a section of map of the coast, marked it with a cross indicating his position and an arrow leading to the village of Phuoc Hai. I also threw in a twenty-four hour ration pack and four cans of Coke that I'd chilled overnight in the mess fridge. I figured the ration pack was enough food to last an Asian a week, and even an Eskimo would recognise the Coke cans. I crammed everything into a sandbag and tied it with string. It now lay on the seat beside me.

That morning I took about twenty minutes to fly to the strip of beach where the old man had set up camp. When I arrived he was standing barefooted in the water, once more gazing out to sea as if expecting a ship to arrive. I noticed he'd collected more crates from along the beach and stacked them all neatly above the tide line. He turned, trudged up from the water and sat down in the shade of his lean-to. I waved. He smiled and waved back. It was almost as if we'd become friends during the past few days. He seemed so old and frail I couldn't believe that he'd survived one day, let alone three. But I'd learned that these people were tough — their life was one long survival exercise, so I guess the old man was running on willpower.

I made a slow pass at about twenty feet. Holding the bag while flying was awkward because the Sioux needed both hands on the controls at low altitude. I threw the bag out and it thumped into soft sand about ten metres from him. I then began circling away.

Cautiously he eyed the sack. I waved to him and pointed, trying to reassure him that it was harmless. He suddenly nodded as if he understood, then bolted across the sand, grabbed it and dashed back to his crates. He quickly untied the string and spilled the contents onto a grass mat. He hobbled back in surprise then turned and looked up at me with a broad grin on his cracked lips. I was risking being shot at by any VC hiding in the jungle fringe but I figured what the hell. I continued to fly slow and low.

The old man clasped his hands under his chin and bowed

slowly. It was such a moving gesture, serene and genuine, that I felt quite humbled. Why were we fighting these people, I wondered. Sure, he wasn't VC, but he *was* Asian. Since I was a child they'd been portrayed as the bad guys. Now I was experiencing something totally at odds with my schooling.

I gave him another wave then climbed away. He picked up a can of Coke, used the clasp knife to punch a hole, then took a long pull. If the Coca-Cola company could have seen him I'm sure their ad people would've signed up the old boy on the spot. He was one happy Chinese.

As I watched I decided to try one more time to convince Task Force HQ. So I climbed to five hundred feet and used the radio. I was told to standby.

I flew south for a few clicks. Near a strip of beach where the jungle was only about twenty metres from the high tide mark I noticed marks in the sand. I dropped down, made a quick pass then climbed away. It looked as though the area had been busy last night; six deep grooves in the sand showed where sampans had come ashore. The ground was covered with footprints leading towards the jungle. I marked my map then climbed higher as Task Force called me.

"Shoot him," the radio operator said bluntly.

I couldn't believe what I was hearing. "Say again?"

"You are to shoot him," Task Force repeated. "Then get identification."

I glanced back up the beach. The old man was standing by the water's edge, gazing out to sea again. Surely someone at Task Force had their wires crossed. He wasn't the enemy.

"You can't be serious!" I complained. "The poor bastard's unarmed!"

"You will shoot him. That is an order." Task Force was adamant.

"I haven't an observer on board," I advised, knowing that would put an end to it. I couldn't fly the aircraft and use a weapon at the same time.

"Confirm you have no observer?"

"Affirmative," I replied, then added: "I'm having difficulty reading you. I'll contact you when I'm on the ground."

I knew I wasn't fooling anyone, so before Task Force could reply, I flicked channels to our flight net, told Ned what had happened, then pointed the nose towards Nui Dat.

NUI DAT

Ned Kelly

When Pedro came up on our flight net, he sounded very pissed off. He wanted to fly back to Nui Dat then storm over to the Task Force CP and strangle someone. I suggested he delay his return for an hour or so by completing the line Bravo recon as scheduled. If Task Force had the hots about kicking his arse for disobeying their order, the delay might allow commonsense to seep into the closeted brain that gave it in the first place. Reluctantly Pedro agreed.

I expected Queeg to be burning up the lines from HQ at any moment. In the last few days the little bugger had started checking on us by working out flight times and distances. If he somehow got wind of the fact we'd been trying to help the old man, the shit would really hit the fan. According to the book, dropping aid to the enemy was strictly *verboten*. But then we were convinced the old man wasn't enemy and by now neither of us really gave a stuff about the book. It was, in our minds, the right thing to do.

I'd just put down the radio handset when the Task Force HQ phone ran. Brown snatched it up. To my relief it was one of Queeg's minions confirming that our standby chopper was required to help with the casualties at Xuyen Moc village. Brown took details of the sortie then checked our flight task board. John Devlin was our standby pilot. He'd been assigned because short timers were only scheduled for the easy jobs: the greatest injustice would be for them to buy the farm with the end in sight. Unfortunately for John, the TET offensive had interfered with this unwritten rule.

I decided to break the news to him personally. I went to our tent, gave him a nudge and briefed him while he rubbed sleep from his eyes. Fortunately the sortie was a passenger run. All he had to do was pick up a nurse and fly her out to Xuyen Moc. As

John hadn't seen a Round Eye woman for almost six months, he was cheered by the prospect. I also knew he'd been chasing pussy at the village and would be concerned about his investment. Ten minutes later he'd cranked up and was heading south.

Lieutenant John Devlin

It was a day I'll never forget. The village of Xuyen Moc east of the Australian Task Force base had been attacked during the night by the Vietcong. My first sortie was to fly a nursing sister from the Australian hospital at Vung Tau out to the village to assist with some of the civilian casualties.

I eased my chopper onto the hospital pad at about 0700hrs and saw a mountain of medical supplies, two orderlies and a petite woman clad in jungle greens standing with an impatient look on her face. Crouching, she sprinted beneath the swooshing blades and clambered into the cockpit.

"You're late!" she shouted as she strapped herself into the right-hand seat.

I'd heard about this woman. She'd been in Vietnam almost ten years, a Catholic nun devoted to the sick and needy — which accounted for about ninety percent of the population. I'd expected her to be an Amazon, with sleeves rolled up and bulging biceps. I was wrong. She was tiny, with a ripe figure her fatigues couldn't disguise. "*You're* Sister Bridget?" I asked with raised eyebrows.

"I am," she called as she clamped the headset over her short blonde hair. Before I could explain how to use the intercom, her voice was loud in my ears. "Get moving, Lieutenant!"

Cautiously I glanced aft to see the orderlies lashing four heavy boxes to each skid pannier. The Sioux is little more than a plastic bubble enclosing three seats bolted to a steel frame. I doubted if I could lift the added weight.

"We're wasting time!" Sister Bridget protested.

I checked the gauges, wound on power and pulled the pitch lever. For all the good it did I might as well have been standing in a bucket tugging the handle. The chopper staggered to a low hover and refused to go any higher.

"Fuck it!" I cursed, not realising I'd instinctively thumbed the intercom button atop the stick.

"What's the problem, Lieutenant?" Sister Bridget taunted me. "I thought you could fly this thing."

I ignored her. The sea breeze was just starting to stretch the windsock so I turned farther into wind then dropped the nose. We rushed across the pad towards a sand dune fringing the beach. At the last moment I tweaked the throttle into overboost and then hauled back the stick. We shot over the dune using its ground effect like a ski ramp. The ground dropped away and we skimmed across the beach into the sun.

I glanced at my passenger. If she was concerned she didn't show it. Disappointed by the lack of applause, I banked low over sampans with fishermen working their nets as they'd done for a thousand years. Some glanced up, most ignored us.

Unable to climb higher than five hundred feet, I skirted a coastal area inhabited by VC with itchy trigger fingers, then headed north. After we settled on course I groped in my pocket for a pack of cigarettes. I shook one out, then holding the stick between my knees, thumbed my battered Zippo and applied the flame.

"I'd like a cigarette," Sister Bridget said suddenly.

Her request took me by surprise. "I didn't know you were allowed," I mumbled as I offered her the pack.

"There's a lot we're not supposed to do," she replied in a reprimanding tone as she lit up.

I suspected her remark was meant to convey some deep spiritual meaning. But my mind was in the gutter, and I wasn't in the mood for sermons — I'd been in the country too long. All I cared about was the next fifteen days. Then my tour would be finished and Vietnam could sink into the South China Sea for all I cared. She could go on healing the sick and raising the dead without my help.

I examined my map, not because I didn't know the way but I needed the diversion. I had a strong feeling Sister Bridget didn't like me — didn't like *any* soldier. She probably had a big silver crucifix stuffed down her shirt which she'd whip out at any moment and thrust before my eyes. *Begone, Satan!*

I squirmed in my seat, tightened my harness, tapped the fuel gauge. The presence of so much righteousness just centimetres away was making me nervous. *Don't blame me for the war, Sister, I only work here!*

I studiously avoided conversation for the next twenty minutes. As we approached Xuyen Moc I circled low and surveyed the damage. Set among rice fields fringed by jungle, the little hamlet had once looked like a Gauguin painting. Now, however, its French nineteenth century church, school and Hotel d'Ville bore the scars of war like the pock marks of a malignant disease. The ARVN outpost on the western boundary was a smoking ruin. A few enemy bodies remained draped over the barbed wire like dirty washing. Five of the thirty Vietnamese soldiers defending the village had been killed. The population of about three hundred were crowded into the village square under the watchful eyes of an ARVN squad.

I'd often visited Xuyen Moc. The village had been adopted by my unit as its civil aid project, part of the Winning Hearts and Minds campaign (known by the acronym WHAM, which was a fitting way of describing the way the Yanks went about it). Six months ago I'd helped rebuild a water pump in the village square. That had taken a lot of sweat and some blood on my part — the result of a steel collar breaking loose from a pipe as we hauled it from the well. It fell from ten feet up, slid down the pipe and wedged around my hands like a giant bracelet. The pain was excruciating but I refused to show it. About twenty villagers were squatting around watching and I wanted to demonstrate the stoicism of their ANZAC saviours. I tried looking nonchalant, as if chunks of steel regularly dropped on me without causing the slightest hurt.

Someone in the crowd sniggered. *'Oc-Da-Loi dinki dow!''* — that means roughly: "This Australian is obviously stupid."

They started laughing. I vowed as soon as I got free I was going to shoot someone. The laughter spread like a plague while two engineers prised the heavy collar from my bleeding hands. By the time I was released I was in the mood to call in an airstrike. I looked around for someone on whom I could vent my anger.

Then I saw her. She was tall for a Vietnamese and I judged there was a touch of French in her parentage. She was about sixteen years old, with small firm breasts pressing against her blue satin *Ow Dai*. The scowl on my face provoked her to more laughter. I turned away and sulked on a pile of sandbags while the medic checked my hands. He assured me the damage was just bruising and cuts, then left me to my misery.

"You okay?" a girl's voice asked. I glanced up to see *her* standing looking at me with a concerned expression. Last thing I wanted was sympathy from a Gook so I ignored her.

She kneeled and stroked my hands. "Number ten," she whispered. "You try to help us and you get hurt." She produced a little banana leaf package from between her breasts and unwrapped it to reveal a pink paste.

"What is that shit?" I asked.

"No sheet! Beetle nut!" Before I could protest she began rubbing it onto my bruised hands. It was fragrant and warm. Weakly I tried to pull my hands away. *Maybe this is some exotic Viet Cong poison,* I thought. *Maybe I'll die bald, cockless and foaming at the mouth.* She gripped my wrists firmly and contiinued applying her folk medicine. "Why you angry at me, GI?" she asked.

"I'm not a Yank," I growled. "I'm Australian."

"*Oc-Dai-Loi* number one," she giggled. "You guys not like them Yankee motherfuckers."

She finished massaging my hands. Suddenly I felt an odd sense of loss. "You got a name?" I ventured as I flexed my fingers. They were stiff and swollen but the pain had eased.

"'Course I got a name. You think I'm a water buffalo or sumpin?" She placed her hands on her hips and slipped a shapely leg forward through the slit in her dress. "My name is Rosie."

"Sure. But what's your real name?"

She flashed an impish grin. "Chay-Yew."

"Hey-You?"

"That near 'nuff." She tilted her head to one side and suddenly became a little girl. She could have been any one of hundreds of kids I knew back home.

"What's your handle?" she asked.

"Audie Murphy," I replied.

"Bullsheet to you! You got your name on your tit there" — she pointed at my name tag. "What's your first name?"

"John."

"You're a Tuee," she laughed as she pronounced the Vietnamese equivalent of Lieutenant. "You take me for a ride in your chopper?" She eased her leg forward again, this time revealing a glimpse of sleek bare thigh and a wisp of fur. "Maybe we join the mile high club?" she teased.

Now that would be interesting, I thought, fascinated by the mechanics of screwing in the Sioux's cramped cockpit. "How old are you?" I asked, feeling very tempted. "And don't try to bullshit me!"

Again she flashed her impish grin. "Fifteen, but I'll soon be twenty-one." She moved her toe in the dust like an Asian Huck Finn. "How old you, Tuee John?"

"Twenty-two," I replied.

"You an old man already," she said as she sat beside me. "Got any gum?"

"No gum." I felt in my shirt pocket and pulled out a tiny bar of soap. It had been sent to me by my parents. A few bars of soap could buy a quick screw in most villages, although I didn't tell that to the folks.

Hey-You took it and our fingers brushed. She smiled. "You want Boom-Boom?"

"No, thank you," I replied, slightly embarrassed by her directness.

"You no like me?" she pouted. "Bet you give plenty jig-a-jig when you go to Vung Tau. Lots of Boom-Boom girls there."

"I'm not based at Vung Tau," I said. "Nui Dat," I pointed west.

"You be my *Oc-Da-Loi* boyfriend, bring more soap?"

"Maybe."

She stood, flicked her long black hair over her shoulder then winked and said in a husky voice, "See you around, honey." She skipped away, leaving me with a curious sense of longing.

Since then I'd dropped into Xuyen Moc whenever time permitted. Being a reconnaissance pilot I was often in the area. Hey-You always greeted me and she'd tag along while we worked on the water pump. The repairs went slowly. Getting parts was almost impossible and we could only work when we were able to round up enough volunteers.

I came to know Hey-You well. Whenever I landed the chopper she'd come over, sit on the skids and talk. Her favourite topic was Australia. She wanted to know what it was like to live in the land of the Big Red Rats — the name the Vietnamese gave to the Kangaroo symbol used on our vehicles and aircraft.

Then there was always the soap. Each time I visited I gave her another piece. I'd written home and asked for more, explaining how it was one way to help improve the health standards of the impoverished Vietnamese. In a rash of missionary zeal my parents spread the word to the local church and soap collecting became a parish obsession.

I rationed the soap — to distribute it all would hve been akin to De Beers releasing their stockpile of diamonds on the world market. The value of soap, like that of diamonds, depending on it remaining a rare commodity. Each visit to Xuyen Moc began with me producing another prettily wrapped bar for Hey-You. She'd turn it end on end and marvel at my generosity. It became a symbol of a bond developing between us. Once I had the notion that I'd fallen in love with her. I dismissed it quickly. In war, maintaining one's perspective is essential. Besides, I rationalised she was probably a VC agent.

Hey-You always wore a spotlessly clean blue satin *Ow Dai*. I suspected it was the only dress she had apart from the shapeless black pajamas she wore in the fields. Whenever I flew in, she'd appear scrubbed and perfumed, dressed in her *Ow Dai*, with a happy smile on her face. How she did it puzzled me.

I solved the mystery one afternoon while delivering mail to the Australian advisors at the village outpost. Just before landing I made a turn that took me over a bend in the creek irrigating the rice fields. There I saw her, splashing naked in the water, her blue dress laid out on a rock. Her black pajamas hung from a tree nearby. Obviously when she heard the distinctive whine of the Sioux's engine she'd sprint from the paddy, scrub up, change quickly then materialise nonchalantly at my side ten minutes later. I was touched that she thought enough of me to go to so much trouble.

I banked away before she saw me. I found it odd that I felt a twinge of guilt at watching her, yet something akin to pleasure whenever I circled a VC position and called down artillery. *Trained to kill, not to love.*

Whenever we talked, our conversation was a mixture of questions and answers, hopes and fears. Sometimes she was a little girl, at others a woman far beyond her tender years. Hey-You laughed a lot, particularly when she tried to come on to me, something she did often. She'd flash those delicious legs, wink and say in a Mae West voice: "Why don't you come up and see me sometime?" I discovered she'd learned English by watching movies and talking to the Americans when she'd lived in Saigon. This explained her repertoire of accents. She could also mimic John Wayne and even produce a passable Cagney accent.

"I want to be a Boom Boom girl. Make lots of money," Hey-You once confided.

Jesus, what an ambition, I thought. *The best this country can offer is for her to aspire to be a whore. What future has she and thousands like her?*

That morning, when I eased the chopper on the pad beside the smouldering outpost, I searched anxiously for Hey-You. I was relieved to see her standing near the water pump, wearing her blue dress.

Before the rotors stopped, Sister Bridget unstrapped, climbed out and began to organise the unloading of her precious supplies. Without even so much as a "thank you", she headed off with a determined stride towards the square. I was grateful to be rid of her.

One of the Australian advisors walked towards me, rifle gripped with the familiar but cautious authority of a veteran combat soldier. "The boss wants to see you in the command bunker." He motioned with one thumb over his shoulder, indicating a sandbagged hole in the ground.

I nodded, pulled off my flying helmet and crammed on my blue beret. As I walked towards the bunker, Hey-You came running to me. She smelled of roses — a contrast to the pungent stinks drifting from the bloating dead as their bodies squeaked and farted in the sun.

"Mighty big fight last night," Hey-You announced. "Bookoo VC. They blow the shit out of Dai-Wee Duc and his men."

Dai-Wee Duc was Captain Duc — he'd commanded the ARVN outpost. I looked to where Hey-You was pointing. Bodies lay under green ponchos, blood pooling, swarms of flies buzzing. Duc had been an arrogant prick who'd enjoyed torturing VC prisoners, especially women. His speciality had been the Hanoi Phone Call: connecting a field telephone to his victim then cranking the handle until they confessed to anything his warped brain dreamed up.

Hey-You saw the satisfied expression on my face. "Dai-Wee Duc numbah-ten," she nodded sagely. "He always try make me go Boom Boom. Say he report me as VC if I didn't. I not do but."

"I know," I replied, perversely happy Duc was now maggot food. "Is your family okay?"

"Sure. We hide while VC attack," she looked up at me. "You gonna find VC now, kill 'em?"

"Maybe," I said as we reached the bunker. "Now you *di-di* back to your mother. Keep your head down until VC all gone. Okay?"

"Okay, Tuee John." She flashed her impish grin. "Aren't you forgetting something?"

I fished in my pocket and pulled out an ivory-and-gold wrapped bar of soap. I tossed it to her. She caught it, then looked wistfully at me. "You always bring me nice present, but I have nothing to give you," she whispered. "Please be careful, Tuee John. Lots of VC out there." She suddenly leapt up and kissed my cheek.

"Damn it, Hey-You. Now beat it," I stammered. *If you let them get to you, you start making mistakes.*

She scurried away and I descended into the bunker. The senior Australian advisor was a craggy faced Warrant Officer who didn't mince words. He was standing at a map tacked to the sandbagged wall. I realised he'd heard me talking with Hey-You.

"Glad you could join us, sir," he said gruffly. "Now if you can spare the time, we've a war to fight." He jabbed the map with his finger. "The VC hit us from two directions last night. For a change our gooks fought well . . ." He flashed me a thin smile. I understood the pressure he was under. Stuck out here, miles from the Task Force, trying to instruct green South Vietnamese soldiers was unrewarding, dangerous work. One never knew which direction the bullets would come from.

". . . Regional ARVN HQ sent us a platoon at first light." He rolled his eyes in exasperation. "I've pushed them out to clear the perimeter, but I'm afraid if they make contact the VC will chew them up. So I need you to recon farther east. If the VC are still around I want to know. We have American long-range artillery on call if you need it." He gave me a look that indicated I was dismissed.

I was glad he was a man of few words. The heat inside the bunker was stifling and there was a stench to the place that made me gag. I quickly marked my map then left. As I trudged towards my chopper I saw Hey-You standing at the edge of the pad. She waved, then ran back across the village square.

I watched her go and turned to the chopper. Suddenly bullets crackled over my head. I dropped on my belly as rounds chewed the dust nearby. I rolled and drew my pistol, then lay cursing the fact I'd left my M-16 in the cockpit.

The firing was coming from the church tower. An M-60 opened up. Red tracer winked across the square. Puffs of concrete dust climbed the wall and bullets clanged off the bell with an unholy pealing.

I saw a figure in the bell tower, one arm tossing a green ball that acred down towards the people huddling near the water pump. There was a flash and a thump as the grenade exploded. The pump tumbled across the ground like a severed head. The M-60 nailed the VC soldier, blew him out of the tower and flung his body into the square.

I heard the distinctive scratch of incoming mortars. I scrambled to my feet, snatched my rifle and ammunition pouch from the cockpit, then dived for cover behind a row of sandbags as malevolent red flowers blossomed across the square. I crawled into an empty weapon pit near the bunker's entrance, cranked a round into my rifle, then popped up and ripped off a magazine on automatic. My tracer floated over the paddy towards the treeline and disappeared harmlessly into the green. It made me feel better so I changed magazines, then lay waiting. The mortars stopped; a grey haze drifted above the square to remind where the rounds had fallen. It was always like this. They fire, we fire, then we all wait while the score is tallied and the next move decided. The insane protocol of war.

Somewhere a woman was screaming. I shut out the confusion around me and squinted up at the sun. It was another stinking hot day. *I'd rather be surfing*, I thought. The beach at Vung Tau was only twenty minutes away by helicopter.

A figure dashed across the square, ignoring shouts to stay down. It was Sister Bridget. She slithered into the pit beside me. "Lieutenant, I need your chopper!" she demanded.

"What the hell?" I muttered. If it had keys I'd have tossed them to her. *Take it, my dear, and gas it up when you've finished.*

"We've six wounded civilians. One is cut bad. If we get her to Vung Tau she has a chance."

"Shit lady, I'm not fitted with litters. Radio for a Dust-Off." No one was going to prise me from the safety of my hole in the ground while the VC were hosing the place with lead, especially to fly a Gook rescue mission. I was a short-timer with only fifteen days to go.

Another burst of fire ripped overhead. I held my rifle tighter, looked ugly, scanned the horizon — anything to avoid looking at *her*.

Sister Bridget ignored my theatrics. "We can prop her in the centre seat. You have to help!"

"Do as the lady says," a voice behind me ordered. I turned to see the Senior Australian Advisor crouched nearby. "We'll put down covering fire while you get airborne. There'll be artillery dropping along the treeline inside a minute."

"I'll meet you at the chopper!" Sister Bridget called as she slipped from the pit and dashed back to the huddle of wailing civilians.

I glanced at the Warrant Officer. The determined look on his face said it all. Even though I out-ranked him, I knew I couldn't refuse. Reluctantly I climbed from my funk-hole then sprinted across the pad and clambered into the chopper. I strapped in, flicked the switches and hit the starter. The engine wheezed, then growled into life.

A new sound joined the confusion: the howl of our artillery arriving. The treeline beyond the paddy spewed earth and fire.

I pulled on my helmet, wrapping myself in a false sense of security. The sounds became muffled. *Like a kid hiding under the blankets during a storm.* I flicked my tinted visor down against the sun's glare, turning the world into a grey monochrome, isolating me further. I was now part of the aircraft, a man-machine, the engine and rotor extensions of my limbs, my brain linked by cable to humming electronics.

Coldly I watched . . .

. . . bloody hands lifting a writhing body into the chopper, strapping her into the centre seat. Blood had darkened the bandages around her belly, chest and head. She looked like a broken toy, hastily repaired . . .

Her eyes snap open and she screams. She tries to fight the bonds holding her arms at her sides, tries to claw her stomach and remove the red hot metal that has invaded her, torn her, *raped* her.

Even above the beating of the rotor and the howl of the engine I hear her screams, pleading, sobbing . . .

I look away and check the gauges.

Sister Bridget straps in, clips a plasma bottle to the bulkhead, its tube snaking into the girl's arm. The radio blurts a message in my ears, drowned by the girl's screams.

"F'Chrissake shut her up!" I shout. "Give her a shot of morphine."

Sister Bridget pulls on her headset and her voice is suddenly loud in my ears. "I can't give her morphine . . . she's got belly, chest and head wounds. Now get this thing up!" she points her index finger in an obscene gesture.

The girl writhes in a renewed burst of agony. Shiny slithers of gut ooze through her blood-soaked dress like escaping snakes. Blood spurts on the seat, pumps in rivers across the floor. I try not to look at her frightened, pleading face. She's saying something to me: "John, John!"

Oh Christ, it's Hey-You! I flick up my visor. The colours return. The blue satin dress is slashed with crimson, her face ghostly pale. She stops screaming and grips me with her dark eyes.

Sister Bridget calls, "Lieutenant, she's got fifteen, maybe twenty minutes before shock kills her." Her voice is emotionless. She knows her business, has figured the odds. But so have I. Fifteen minutes to cover almost forty kilometres. It can't be done, not in this antique. But I must try.

I slam my visor down, then wind on power. The Sioux staggers up, falters, then seems to gather strength. I drive the boost needle into the red, but all we can manage is a six-foot hover. The heat of the day has thinned the air, sapping the engine's power and depriving the rotors of lift. I curse the politicians for sending us to war with outdated aircraft: here I am spinning like a blowfly in a jar while a little girl bleeds her life away.

I notice that a breeze has sprung up from the east. It will have to be another running take-off, but this time over an enraged enemy and through incoming artillery.

"Check fire! Check fire!" I shout over the radio as I line up on the explosions blocking our take-off path.

"Negative, negative," crackles the reply. "My One-Four is in contact!"

"Move this thing, Lieutenant!" Sister Bridget yells.

"Jesus lady, we can't fly through that." I protest as another salvo lands. *Whump-whump-whump*! Dust hangs like an impenetrable red curtain, two hundred metres in front of us.

"This kid is dying, Lieutenant! Move it!"

Time the salvos. Six guns firing. Reload, ten seconds, resight five seconds. Time of flight . . . who knows? Catch the gap!

Whumpa-whump-whump!

"Go!" I scream, and dip the nose. The Sioux bolts, whipping out over the paddy into flickering streams of tracer. I start counting. One, two, three. We swoop low over a VC squad who start firing at us. Four, five six. A bullet drills a jagged hole in the cockpit in front of me. Seven, eight, nine. We're into the dust and smoke, flying blind. Thirteen, fourteen . . .

Whump-whump-whump.

The chopper shakes from the blasts but they're *behind* us. We break through the dust cloud, climbing slowly. A final crackle of bullets, then we're over the jungle, hugging the trees. A leaf from a splintered rubber tree flutters into the cockpit, oozes white latex that mixes with the blood.

Hey-You has stopped screaming. I sneak a look and see her eyelids are drooped. I glance at Sister Bridget. Her fingers lift to Hey-You's neck, find her pulse. She adjusts the drip then says: "Just fly this thing, Lieutenant, let me worry about her."

I look away, check the flight instruments. The aircraft is flying normally, gauges in the green except for the boost needle which quivers on the red zone. I thumb the transmit button and speak. "Two niner, this is Possum Two Three, leaving your push and going Pork Pie." *Who thinks these names up?* I wonder as I flick the channel selector. I briefly eavesdrop on other dramas on other stages, reminding me I'm not the only player in this insane war. In other places, other people are dying too.

I call on the hospital frequency. "Pork Pie, I'm inbound. Have figures one, Whiskey-India-Alpha on board." *Will I ever be able to carry on a normal conversation again?*

I look at Sister Bridget and point to the radio. She nods, pushes her transmit button and rattles off a stream of medical jargon. The hospital acknowledges. A team will be waiting on the pad.

I check Hey-You. Her eyes flicker open and she looks up at me. An impish grin quivers on her lips then her head slumps against my shoulder. I can feel her breath warm through my flying suit. At least she's alive, but for how long? I sneak a questioning glance at Sister Bridget. She points ahead. "Just fly Lieutenant, *fly!*" There's anger in her voice.

Vung Tau creeps onto the horizon. A squall moves in from the sea. We punch through it, rain streaking the canopy and soaking my left side. My right shoulder feels cold. Has she stopped breathing? I look. Her eyes flicker and she smiles weakly.

A red cross against white marks the pad. I circle the hospital then drop down, skids clunking on the concrete.

Faces and hands, white coats and stretcher bearers become a blur. Hey-You is bundled out and whisked away before I can unplug the umbilical that makes me part-machine.

The rotor stills. I secure the aircraft and walk through the driving rain towards the long silver buildings. Strange smells, *clean* smells, invade my nostrils, contrasting against the stink of cordite, sweat and shit of the real world just minutes away. My boots squeal on polished vinyl, announce that I'm an intruder.

"Where'd they take her?" I confront an orderly.

"Wait, sir," he replies and walks through flapping doors. I wait.

"Lieutenant," a voice calls from a brightly lit corridor. Sister Bridget stands in a bloodstained gown, surgical mask around her neck. "She's dead," she announces flatly. No apologies, no explanations.

I walk towards her, trying to find some logic, grasp some meaning. Hey-You was just a kid who got in the way — was killed by her own people. *Or was she?*

Sister Bridget's stare frightens me. She's worked in this sausage machine too long, become conditioned by the triage. Deciding who lives and who dies has sapped her humanity. She's not an angel of mercy, she's Satan in drag. I look into her eyes and I see my own reflection.

"You got a problem Lieutenant?" she demands. "She was ony a Gook. Isn't that what you guys call them?"

"Sure," I reply. "She was only a Gook." I turn, suddenly wanting to run away from this sterile factory, back to the real world of pain and killing.

"Lieutenant!" Sister Bridget calls as I reach the door.

I stop and look back at her. She comes forward and pauses five paces from me. "Here!" She tossed me a tiny square object.

I catch it and see it is a bar of soap, blood still moist on the wrapper.

"Your *friend* wanted you to have it," Sister Bridget whispers. She turns and walks away.

"The army's supply system is very easy to understand — provided one believes in miracles." Captain Paul "Paddy" O'Brien, 161 Rotary Wing Section commander, Sept 1967-Sept 68

0730HRS

Ned Kelly

At Nui Dat we were only vaguely aware of the action John Devlin was involved in. He'd checked in on our flight net and advised us he was taking a casualty to the Australian Field Hospital at Vung Tau, then flicked to their frequency. We knew he'd report when he'd compleed the sortie, so we thought nothing of it.

Pedro was stretching his recon as much as his fuel would allow. He'd soon return, gas up and after a quick break get back out. I hadn't heard a peep from Queeg, so I figured whatever had gone on between Pedro and HQ could be put down to temporary insanity. Queeg would be only too happy to fry one of our pilots for disobeying orders, and so far he'd not mentioned the incident. But something in the back of my mind told me the matter wasn't forgotten. I had the feeling that Task Force HQ was like a volcano waiting to erupt, eerily silent before the explosion.

I roamed the CP trying to look busy while Dave Brown leaned back in his folding chair, flipping through the pages of a dog-eared motor-bike magazine. Bikes were his passion and he was saving his pay to buy the latest Japanese creation when he returned to Australia.

I scanned the logbook, noticing one item still outstanding. The windsock at the western end of the runway was now a bleached rag, drooping from its pole like a flag of defeat. It undoubtedly gave the enemy the impression we were sloppy housekeepers so I'd put in a request to our Quartermaster for a replacement. That was almost a month ago. Asking him when it would arrive had become a morning ritual.

I dreaded crossing swords with our QM. Apart from being too crafty to be outwitted by a mere lieutenant, he was ex-Welsh Guards and had a glass eye. Looking at him firmly when being assertive (as per the officer training manual) was impossible. I always ended up focussing on the tip of his nose and fluffing my lines. Reluctantly I picked up the phone, cranked the handle and was switched through to the QM's empire.

"Ahar, Staff Sergeant Shorrock speaking," the QM answered in a booming voice.

I went for the jugular. "QM, where's our new windsock?"

"Zur, we still be waiting for one to come in from Australia."

"I thought a shipment arrived yesterday?" In my mind's eye I pictured the bulbous red tip of his nose.

"It did, zur, but they sent us twelve dozen pairs of socks-khaki instead of a socks-wind."

Quartermasters spoke the way the supply manual read: item name first, description last. This was confusing enough, but with Shorrock's thick accent it was like talking to a retarded pirate. "How did that happen?" Too late I realised I shouldn't have asked.

"Well, zur, seeing that aviation be new to the h'army, the supply depots back in Australia probably aren't carrying socks-wind yet. So they sent us the next best thing, socks-khaki, woollen, soldiers-for-the-use-of. We needed them anyway. Har, har!"

I searched futilely for an answer, but my imagination conjured up two vast caves created by his flaring nostrils. All I could manage was a frustrated: "But, but —"

"I can give you a ripper deal on socks-khaki, zur," the QM chuckled. "These 'uns be pure wool."

I wondered if we should hang a few around the fields-air. It would give the base, Dats-Nui, a look, domestic. "Very funny, QM." I dug my heels in. "But, we urgently need a new socks-wind, pilots-for-the-judging-of-the-breeze! Preferably a red one."

"Zur, I provides only what the system is prepared to cough up."

"Look, QM, if the bloody Viet Cong see that we can't replace a torn windsock, they'll get the impression we're short of equipment. Then they'll start getting ideas!"

"That could be a worry I admit. Those slopeheads be crafty devils. Reminds me of Kenya —"

"Just get on it, will you, QM?" I was in no mood for Shorrock's recounting of the Mau-Mau uprisings. His were shocking sagas of rape, bestiality and cannibalism — and that was how the good guys passed their time.

"Leave it to me, zur!"

"Okay, and save me six pairs of socks-khaki."

"I can only let you have three, zur. They're going fast, har-har!"

"Whatever." I put the phone down, grateful to have escaped the world of piratical back-speak. "That man needs an enema," I muttered, attempting to gloss over yet another lost round with Shorrock. It wasn't good for my image. Officer training should include the handling, care and feeding of crafty one-eyed NCOs.

"The QM's already got a new windsock," Brown announced as he looked up from his magazine. "I saw it hidden in the back of the Q-Store."

"He has? Then why won't he hand it over?"

"Shorrock figures if he gave it to us, then he'd have none in store if we wanted one in an emergency."

Of course! I thought. How sublimely logical — why didn't I think of that? Besides, the pilots could use the smoke from the rubbish dump adjoining the airfield for a wind indicator as they'd been doing for the last six months.

I struck the windsock from the log: so much for impressing the neighbours. I slumped in one of the canvas chairs and brooded at the wall map. I wondered what Charlie was up to in those neat green squares. Was their supply system as whacko as ours? I hoped so. If it wasn't, we were doomed.

I glanced up at the Task Force Intelligence report. It hung from its clipboard like a vulture waiting to pounce. If a North Vietnamese regiment was moving into Phuoc Tuy province, surely we could locate them. A regiment was more than two thousand men and that was a lot of soldiers to hide, even for the chameleon-like VC. But then there was a lot of jungle for them to hide in — despite attempts to strip the country bare with defoliants. If the NVA Regiment linked up with the VC battalions we knew were already out there, that would make a total of over six thousand enemy dedicated to our destruction. The rule of thumb was for an attacking force to have at least a three-to-one advantage. With only about two thousand of us left at Nui Dat, the ratio would be in the enemy's favour.

I could remember the fifties era when Reds-Under-the-Bed and The Screaming Yellow Hordes were Australian politicians' favourite bogey men. Now my worst childhood fears looked as if they were about to be realised. I pictured swarms of VC filtering ant-like through the jungle towards Nui-Dat. The definitive Yellow Horde — and Reds bot boot. My heart sank.

To depress my mood further, Armed Forces Radio introduced General Westmoreland giving one of his pep talks:

"American soldiers and brave Allies," Westy began. "Let me tell you that your efforts and sacrifices during this treacherous Communist offensive . . ."

Like a bad smell, Westmoreland had the ability to be everywhere at once. With the subtlety of a laxative commercial, he'd pop up on Armed Forces Radio or television, using Mom and Apple Pie rhetoric in an attempt to intimidate his audience into feeling noble about dying for the cause. It certainly didn't wash with us and I wondered how effective he thought he was amongst his own troops. I think if he'd gone out and asked, he would've been one very surprised little general.

I ignored his prattling. Instead, I pulled out my pistol and began cleaning it. Somehow it made me feel better.

TAN SON NHUT AIRPORT, SAIGON, 0800HRS

Mike Dawson

We'd been sitting around the tarmac for more than two hours. During this time we'd seen two USAF C-141s come and go, each one delivering fresh troops to be welcomed by the flag-waving, bugle-blowing reception committee — then loading up and shipping out frozen corpses. It wasn't good for my morale.

Twice a RAAF Caribou landed and picked up groups for the Vung Tau logistics base, leaving us waiting. Eventually the rotund Air Force Sergeant returned in his lopsided jeep to let us know there were delays with aircraft due to enemy action. By now we'd nicknamed the fat oaf "Blimpy".

"The TET offensive," Blimpy clucked. "It's big, damned big."

Having been shut off from the world for more than twenty-four hours, for all we knew the VC might have overrun the entire country by now. Blimpy waved a flacid hand towards the distant rice fields and informed us that he knew very little about what was going on, *out there*. All he was concerned with was his little empire. But were we going to be shipped to Nui Dat merely to return a few hours later in a refrigerated box? He made it clear that wasn't his worry.

Blimpy hauled an urn of iced water from the back of the jeep and put it in the shade near the revetment. He pointed to a distant terminal, telling us to use it if we felt the call of nature. "But be careful," he warned. "Last night VC suicide squads got through the airfield perimeter. Might be a few still left roaming around." The jeep's springs groaned as he climbed aboard. "I'll check on you later," he called as he drove off.

We needed little encouragement to stay put. We weren't armed — our weapons would be issued when we arrived at our units. None of us had the inclination to bump into a VC suicide squad and join the legions of frozen warriors parading past us on their journey to Valhalla.

Being the only officer in my group I found myself in charge. The next time Blimpy appeared, I tried to pin him down about when our aircraft would arrive. All he could say was that it would be any minute now. He then muttered something about morning tea, squeezed into his creaking jeep and sped away.

We settled back in the shade of the revetment to wait. Some managed to doze despite the clamour, stretched out on the hot concrete with their heads on their duffle bags. All I could do was to sit impatiently, reflecting on the fact that what they say about war is true: it's ninety per cent boredom. I couldn't help being a little worried by the prospect of the other ten per cent.

The Bin Gia SNAFU
NUI DAT
Ned Kelly

By 0800hrs activity was increasing. One chopper was flying a Voice Mission — using loudspeakers to convince the enemy they should surrender — while one fixed-wing and one helicopter were on Province recon. Queeg was constantly on the phone, pushing me to ask the pilots if they'd found anything. I knew if our pilots did find anything unusual they'd advise us immediately. Constantly coming up on the radio to ask them served no purpose. In fact, for the pilot it was time consuming and dangerous: although our transmitter had enough power to reach *them*, they'd have to climb to almost five hundred feet to answer our call. That placed the aircraft in small-arms range of any VC who happened to be watching. It was difficult to get this message across to those unfamiliar with aircraft operations.

To satisfy Queeg's incessant curiosity, Dave Brown and I established a ruse that was something akin to a vaudeville act. Task Force HQ didn't monitor our flight net, so when Queeg demanded we question our aircraft (providing it was what we judged a nuisance request) we'd simulate a radio call complete with background engine noise provided by a battery powered razor. That way we kept everyone happy. In fact we became so proficient at aircraft imitations, in slack periods we'd come up on our control tower frequency and put the controller through torment with approaches by non-existent aircraft. In a few weeks we'd convinced him his eyesight was failing.

That morning though, Queeg fired so many queries at us that by 0800hrs the batteries in my razor had expired. I was about to change them when the phone from Task Force jangled urgently.

"Lieutenant, contact your voice aircraft immediately!" Queeg demanded. "I want to know what he thinks he's doing!"

I fumbled with the batteries and they spilled onto the ground. "Damn!" I swore.

"What's that?" Queeg yelled.

"I said, I'm trying now, sir." I muffled the phone's handpiece and looked at Dave Brown. "What's the voice aircraft's mission?" I whispered.

Brown checked the task board. "A sortie over Binh Gia village. Should be returning any minute now."

There was something about Queeg's tone that made me play for time. "Sir, we're having trouble raising him at the moment, can I call you back in five?"

"Make it snappy Lieutenant!" Queeg hung up.

"Better raise the voice aircraft on the flight net," I ordered Brown. I was suspicious — my instinct told me something was amiss. But what could go wrong with a Voice Mission f'Christ sake?

Most people are familiar with the loudspeaker-equipped Hueys in the movie *Apocalypse Now*. But contrary to the image created by F.F. Coppola, the function of such aircraft wasn't to lead the air cavalry into battle with Wagnerian accompaniment. Instead they were intended for use in Psychological Warfare Operations (Psyops) against the VC. Voice Missions (VMs) were supposed to lower the enemy's morale and make them surrender *en masse*. This was part of the Chieu Hoi or Open Arms program — another misguided weapon of the Vietnam War. Special music was compiled by Task Force Intelligence featuring the voices of sultry Oriental maidens pleading to the misguided VC to dash home to the wife or girlfriend (or both) for a quickie. To use these tapes sounded like the clash of saucepans and the cry of waitresses in a Chinese take-away. So none of us had a clue what was being broadcast.

In fact, Voice Missions had become a source of entertainment. The Americans regularly flew a speaker-equipped fixed-wing aircraft over the Task Force and serenaded us by playing Mitch Miller and gang singing *Waltzing Matilda* in the belief it was our National Anthem. This inspired us to record our own collection, which included the Beatles, Slim Dusty and Rolph Harris. It became customary for a pilot returning from a voice mission to make a few circuits of the base while playing one of these tapes.

As expected, shortly after his arrival Queeg declared this behaviour unmilitary. No one at Task Force HQ had objected before, in fact the practice had been tacitly encouraged as a morale booster. One of Queeg's staff let slip that his chief liked brass band music, so we added a few stirring military marches to the program and ignored his edict.

Today's sortie had been scheduled by Task Force as the start to a battalion Cordon and Search operation. I rechecked the briefing sheet sent to us by Task Force Intelligence. It was all straightforward: *Fly to village Xa Bingh Gia, be on station at first light and play tape until advised to cease.* Piece of cake.

Lieutenant Glen Duus was tasked for the sortie. Glen had been a little pissed off at having to fly yet another voice sortie over Binh Gia; we'd been serenading this particular village for several weeks with the standard heartthrob compositions. To our knowledge no one had yet turned themselves in. We figured that by now any VC in the area had been tipped off that an operation was imminent and cleared out to join their pals in the action around Saigon. Why the grunts were now going to cordon and search the place was a mystery to us. However, ours wasn't to reason why. Glen clattered into the pre-dawn sky on schedule. Ten minutes later he reported he was over the village:

> "When I arrived over Binh Gia I circled at about six hundred feet looking for the infantry that was supposed to be surrounding the village, but I couldn't see any sign of them — it was too dark. I knew if I sprung the operation without the battalion in position, Charlie would be off like a shot and I'd be left standing in front of the fan. So I checked my Signals Instructions, found the battalion's HQ frequency and called them up on the radio. Because we knew Charlie was always listening I used suitably veiled speech, saying something like: "This is Possum Two-Four, I'm in position, can I start?" After a pause a sleepy Australian voice replied. "Er . . . um . . . okay, Possum." So I went ahead and played the tape. I circled until I was low on fuel then headed for Nui Dt. On the way back, our CP came on the horn. I could tell by Ned's voice that something had gone wrong."

I had a horrible premonition as Dave Brown raised Glen on the radio then handed me the microphone. Glen confirmed he was inbound to Nui Dat. "Anything unusual about the sortie?" I ventured. I knew it seemed an odd question — normally Psyops tapes produced little reaction apart from an occasional bullet through the aircraft from the less appreciative members of the audience.

"Now that you mention it, there was," Glen replied tersely.

Uh-oh, I thought. *What's screwed up now?*

Glen continued, his voice shuddering in rhythm with the vibrating helicopter. "I played the tape and everyone in the village came out as if they were waiting for a visit from Santa Claus. Trouble was I couldn't see any of our grunts around the village."

That was unusual, I thought. The grunts were normally on the ball. But who knew what Task Force Intelligence was up to? They loved secrecy. Maybe this was a plot to frustrate the VC into surrendering.

Glen then advised he was approaching the circuit. He left the flight net and called the tower. A few minutes later I heard his aircraft over the field. He'd selected one of our tapes for the traditional serenade and was circling around at about a thousand feet playing *Tie Me Kangaroo Down Sport*. As the Doppler twisted *woop-woop* of Rolph Harris's wobble board boomed down from the sky, the phone from Task Force HQ almost leapt off the wall.

"Possum Control," I answered.

"This is Seagull speaking!" the phone blasted.

Damn! I'd forgotten about Queeg. I snapped to attention, tugged at my forelock and replied: "Yessir! What can I do for you?"

"Lieutenant, what the hell is that bloody voice helicopter doing?"

I figured Queeg was bitching about Rolph Harris. I gave the standard reply. "Testing the amplifiers sir! We have the Band of the Welsh Guards playing *Men of Harlech* in the next bracket."

The phone sizzled. "You blithering idiot! Not Rolph Harris, the tape your pilot played over Binh Gia. *The operation isn't due until tomorrow!*"

Oh shit! So that's why Glen couldn't see the grunts! They were still back at Nui Dat. Looks as if we'd prematurely kick-started a campaign that had been planned to catch Uncle Ho on his annual pep-tour of the colonies. Being versed in the ways of tin-plating my arse, I gave the stock reply. "Standby one."

I needed time to think. Obviously there'd been a mammoth screw-up somewhere. When these occur the first rule of survival is to blame someone else. I knew if Queeg found the slightest chink in our armour the little bastard would pounce on it with glee: probably demand that I be put in front of a firing squad, or worse, sent to the infantry as a platoon commander. I needed somewhere or someone to point the figure at *fast*. This was definitely a case of the quick and the dead.

I cranked the phone to the tower and asked the controller to have Glen come up on the flight net. In a few seconds he was on the horn. I explained what had happened. Fortunately Glen confirmed that the instruction on the envelope containing the offending tape specified today's date. Seems someone at Task Force Int had goofed by putting the wrong tape in the envelope. When he made his radio call to the battalion's HQ he had no way of knowing it was still at Nui Dat. As I later discovered, the battalion's duty radio operator was nearing the end of a long night shift, and when Glen asked permission to proceed, not having a clue what was going on, the soldier figured the safest reply was a quick "yes".

This information was enough to checkmate Queeg. I passed it on and I imagined him squirming as he realised he had to find somewhere else to apply the heat. I was off the hook. The incident demonstrated how easily a meticulously planned operation could come unglued through human error.

After a few minutes the phones went berserk as other HQ staff officers demanded explanations in an effort to make sure *their* arses were covered. I pictured Queeg running around like a fox in a chicken coop in his search for someone to crucify. I let Dave Brown handle the avalanche of inquiries while I collapsed in a seat and shook with laughter. In the background Rolph Harris was still booming down from the sky.

Greatcoats on . . . greatcoats off . . .
Ned Kelly

It was around 0900hrs when John Devlin returned from his Vung Tau medivac sortie. He reported in on our flight net, then a few minutes later I heard his chopper land on the maintenance pad and shut down.

I was standing at the wall map, marking the latest recon sightings when John stormed into the CP. In one hand his flying helmet dangled by its chin strap, in the other he gripped his M-16. He stood near the door, staring at me with a wild look in his eye. He threw his helmet at the map. It slammed into the Nui Thi Vi hills, bounced onto the floor and lay rocking to and fro. He dropped his rifle, went to my chrome microphone, seized it and shouted: *"Fuck Vietnam!"* He then strode off towards his tent like a bear with a sore tooth.

Dave Brown watched him go, shrugged, then continued reading his magazine. I picked up John's rifle, removed the magazine and worked the action. A cartridge flicked across the CP and clanged onto the floor. I could smell burned cordite. I put the weapon in the rack, figuring it would be best to keep it away from John until he'd cooled down.

Temper outbursts were common from our pilots. Often I was the first point of contact and bore the brunt. Nothing ever came of it except that I usually received a few beers as a peace offering during the evening drinking session. I think fifty per cent of the booze I consumed in Vietnam was acquired this way.

I thought nothing more of John's show of affection for Vietnam until a few minutes later when the Engineering Officer walked into the CP.

Engineering Officers — Engos — are sensitive people. Ours was almost distraught: it was a matter of honour with him to keep our aircraft flying. He explained that John's helicopter had fifteen bullet holes and a dozen shrapnel hits in its skeletal airframe — not bad shooting, considering it was mostly welded pipe and vacant space. Six of the hits were in the rotor blades and they would have to be replaced.

The fact that the enemy had maliciously damaged one of the Engo's precious birds was a personal affront to him. The tone of his voice reflected the depth of his distress: "The cockpit needs to be washed out, the floor and seats are covered in blood." He was verging on tears. (How dare anyone *bleed* in one of my aircraft!) "And we'll have to change the bubble when the fucking supply system gets around to sending us a new one!"

"How long before it's serviceable again?" I asked.

"Depending on what other damage we find . . . working flat out, three . . . maybe four hours." He turned, snatched up our fake microphone and barked: "Fuck Vietnam!" The act calmed him. He smiled at me, then headed back to the hangar.

That left us one aircraft short. I was curious to find out what had happened — and I needed an explanation for Task Force. I figured John would have cooled off by now so I picked up his helmet and went to our tent.

John was lying on his bunk. "I've finished with this fucked-out war," he snapped as I entered. "Take me off the flight schedule. I'm not budging from here for the next fourteen days."

I could see he was in no mood for conversation. I put his helmet at the foot of his bunk and left him staring at the canvas roof.

Back in the CP I checked the task board. Ross Hutchinson would have to take John's place on the flight schedule. He'd just finished a two week stretch as duty officer, the result of the Army's strangely warped sense of justice that dictated if a crime was committed, someone must pay. Hutch's felony had been nothing more sinister than failing to get a truckload of our soldiers back from Vung Tau before the evening curfew. Prior to the TET offensive, Task Force units were allowed to send leave parties to the Vung Tau R&R Centre on Sundays. They'd carouse in the bars and clubs or swim at the beach until mid-afternoon before setting off back to Nui Dat. Hutch's group had clambered aboard the truck for the return trip but, surprise, surprise, as they were rolling through the village of Cat-Lo, about ten clicks south of Nui Dat, the truck suffered unexplained engine failure. It drifted to a halt outside the First National Massage Parlor.

Fifteen soldiers scattered. There followed a Max Sennet comedy as Hutch flushed his charges from room to room in an attempt to round them up. He finally gave in. As he later admitted: "The sight of all that thrashing pussy finally got to me. I threw away caution and dived in at the deep end."

The leave truck arrived back at Nui Dat after dark, having been miraculously repaired before running the gauntlet up Route Two at high speed. The incident was hardly his fault, but as Hutch was in charge of the group he wore the discipline on the personal order of the Task Force Commander. (After two more similar engine failures, the truck was found to have a hot-wired ignition switch beneath the driver's seat).

The annoying result was that we were one pilot down for the term of his punishment. Although our OC tried to have the penalty lifted because it affected our operational capability, the Task Force commander insisted that justice be seen to be done. We partly circumvented the order by filling in for Hutch whenever we could, but El Supremo soon pinged to this and ordered our OC to ensure that Hutch was on duty twenty-four hours a day for the duration — no ifs or buts. He also added another week for good measure. From then on the Brigadier took a personal interest in seeing the sentence was carried out. He'd have one of his staff officers check up daily, and occasionally he'd drop into our CP unannounced to verify for himself that Hutch was still serving his time.

By the end of his term Hutch's eyeballs were dropping out. So when I told him he would have to replace John he was less than excited. But he knew John wouldn't have called it a day without good reason. Hutch wouldn't be needed until John's aircraft was repaired, but to his credit he saddled up and made himself ready.

I rechecked the flight schedule. Two helicopters had been assigned to continual surveillance, looking for signs of preparations for an attack on the base. Pedro Taylor had returned and his aircraft was being refuelled. He'd be ready to go again in a few minutes. The only other aircraft available to fill in was the voice chopper. With the heavy speaker gear on board it was a deathtrap at low level.

I felt a perverse sense of exitement. This news would disrupt Queeg's plans. He'd been currying favour by sending senior staff officers on joy rides around the Province — two were lined up for the standby aircraft later in the day. These would now have to be scrubbed. I resented his intrusion into my realm, because joy flights were a racket that I was riding very nicely. For one American poncho liner (which I used as currency for further trade) I'd get anyone a seat on a Province recon. Queeg's brown-nosing had cut my takings by fifty per cent.

I cranked the phone and Queeg came on the line. He'd

calmed since I last spoke to him: obviously finding the villain behind the voice-mission fiasco had scored him plenty of points with the Task Force honchos. I knew when I told him the standby aircraft was temporarily out of action he'd go off the deep end.

"Yes Lieutenant, what is it?" he demanded.

I told him we were now one aircraft short, possibly for the next six hours. I figured by exaggerating the time for repair, its return to serviceability after four hours or less would make us look good.

Queeg was livid. His voice rose to fever pitch as he cross-examined me on how John's aircraft had been damaged. I explained briefly, then added: "There is a war on, you know!" I thought maybe he hadn't noticed.

"Don't give me lip!" he snapped.

Lip? I hadn't heard that expression since I was a kid at school. I held the phone out so Dave Brown could listen in. Queeg demanded a full report be sent to Task Force. I promised to do it immediately (with the intention of forgetting about it the moment I put down the phone) ". . . and you're to maintain the reconnaissance schedule," he concluded.

"The only way we can do that is by removing the equipment from the voice aircraft," I advised him. "Does Int want to use it again today?"

"No! The damned thing's caused enough trouble already!" Queeg growled. "The recon schedule must be maintained. Take the speakers off and use it!" He hung up in my ear.

"This place is shitting me," I muttered to Dave Brown.

"Don't let him get to you," he calmly replied.

I cranked the phone to the Engo and asked him to have the speaker gear removed from the voice aircraft. He said doing it meant taking manpower from repairing John's aircraft. I told him the trade-off was necessary — at least we'd have an aircraft available within half an hour. He said they'd get right on it.

To my surprise Queeg's phone rang again. "Before you remove that speaker gear we've one more sortie for the aircraft," Queeg blurted. "The population of Binh Gia are still standing around the village square like statues. We're sending over a translator who'll tell them they can disperse." *(Click.)*

Damn you! I thought as I reached for the Engo's phone. "Hold that order to remove the speaker gear!" I yelled.

"Listen Ned, make up yer fucking mind," the Engo complained. "Do you want it on, or off?"

"Definitely on!" I replied. "Take it off after the next sortie."

"Next sortie?"

I explained.

"That's great," the Engo protested. "We were just taking a few parts to fit to John's aircraft."

"What parts?"

"Only some bits the system hasn't come good with yet," he replied.

That was typical of our supply system, I thought. Shortage of parts, particularly UHF radios, had become so acute that our ground crew had taken to scrounging them from American aircraft refuelling at Nui Dat. They'd create a diversion, then while the aircrew was occupied they'd rip out a flight instrument or radio and replace it with one of our defunct components. The Yanks would flutter away, none the wiser until they tried using the purloined item. As it was a simple matter for them to have it replaced within minutes at the nearest US base, the effect of our ground crew's kleptomanic behaviour on the US war effort was minimal. (At least that was the rationale.)

"Just as well you caught us now and not in ten minutes time," the Engo added. He hung up, leaving me wondering what "bits" they'd had their beady eyes on.

As I put the Engo's phone down, Queeg's clamoured for attention. Reluctantly, I put it to my ear. Queeg kicked off without any introduction. "And another thing Lieutenant, seeing that your first light reconnaissance found signs of enemy activity along the coast, I want the area checked out further. I'm sending a *reliable* Staff Officer to act as observer on the next sortie."

He hung up again. No goodbye or thank you. I contemplated shooting the phone but the prospect of the paperwork that would result from malicious destruction of military property put me off. I gave it a Nazi salute instead.

"Task Force must be getting the jitters," Dave Brown replied when I told him what Queeg wanted. "Something's brewing," he added with a satisfied look. "Something big."

Reluctantly I agreed with him. The problem was that when Task Force HQ got it into their heads the sky was falling in, the pressure on us increased. Panicking was their job, I rationalised.

I looked around for Pedro. I knew he'd be overjoyed at the prospect of having a staff officer as passenger on his next sortie. I found him in the mess trying to prise a mummified rat from inside the toaster. So that's why the bread was tasting better lately.

Pedro Taylor

I landed back at Nui Dat around 0830hrs and shut down. After leaving the old man I'd continued around line Bravo and, apart from the marks on the beach where the sampans had come ashore, I'd found nothing.

While my chopper was being refuelled I went to our CP, filed my report, then headed for the mess to grab a bite to eat. Seems Task Force HQ had forgotten about my refusal to obey orders — either sanity had returned to Bullshit Castle or they'd become occupied with something else. (When Ned told me about the voice mission screw-up, I understood why.) But my smugness was short lived. Ned also told me that Task Force HQ had decided to send a staff officer to act as observer during my next sortie. They wanted to see for themselves where the VC had come ashore during the night.

This was a sore point with us. Task Force always seemed reluctant to acknowledge that we were capable of detecting signs of enemy activity. I'd been in country almost eight months and flown around the Province daily. When I first arrived in Vietnam it had taken me about a week to familiarise myself with the area. It was another week or so before I'd actually learned to find things and be useful as a reconnaissance pilot.

I now knew Phuoc Tuy Province like the back of my hand, but despite continual explanations to Task Force, they still didn't understand that it took time to train a competent observer. Simply taking a staff officer and strapping a helicopter to his bum didn't qualify him: you had to learn how to see through the jungle canopy and interpret apparently insignificant signs. It was like the skills a black tracker learns that enable him to follow his quarry over imposible terrain. Those skills weren't gained from a manual.

No matter how often we tried to explain, Task Force HQ believed the only way our findings could be verified was for Staff Officers to take a look. It was as if eyesight was proportional to rank. I could understand if it was to oversee a raging battle, or if staff officers could recognise what they were looking at, but too often all they were doing was taking joy flights.

It was 1030hrs when the staff officer arrived. I'd been sitting around cooling my heels waiting and felt somewhat antagonistic towards him. He was an artillery Major who'd been in country two weeks; this was his first flight around the Province. To be fair to him, he seemed a reasonable type — he sensed my antipathy and admitted it was ridiculous that he'd been sent to verify ski-marks and a few footprints in the sand.

With the air cleared a little, I showed him how to strap in and use the intercom. I then cranked up and fifteen minutes later we were flying over the beach. The Major sat with his M-16 across his knee, its muzzle pointed out of the right hand side of the cockpit. I flew north along the jungle fringe until I came to the area where I'd found the keel marks during my first light recon.

I circled low. The grooves were still firm in the moist sand. I pointed out a trail of footprints leading from the water's edge towards the jungle a hundred metres away. They were deep, which meant men carrying heavy loads. And they went in both directions: back and forth movement indicated teams transferring a large cargo.

I risked coming to a hover and indicated how the VC had been careful to tread in the preceding set of footprints. This made it difficult to assess exactly how many men had come ashore. It also minimised their risk of stepping on land mines (some areas of beach farther south had been mined by the South Vietnamese Army — all they'd succeeded in doing was maiming a few local fishermen and their children). It also showed they were disciplined. I estimated maybe fifty or more enemy had been involved.

For almost an hour we searched the area, following the tracks into the jungle and finding more signs of overnight activity. Then, drawn by an irresistible curiosity about the old man, I headed back to the coast. Over the beach I turned north, flying low over the water's edge. As we flew I surveyed the waves with a critical eye. Back home I'd been raised on Queensland's Gold Coast where I'd spent many of my teenage years surfing. Before being conscripted I'd owned a rusting Holden panel van and cruised the beaches. It seemed so long ago, yet I realised it was only two years. I felt a sudden anger at having been plucked from my carefree existence then thrust into a world whose only purpose seemed to be to inflict suffering.

I glanced at my passenger. I wondered what was going through his mind. He sensed my gaze and looked at me. "It's a bloody shame we have to fight here," the Major said over the intercom. He smiled thinly. Maybe I'd misjudged career officers; this guy seemed to have a heart.

"I was told you've been observing someone around here," he said suddenly.

I nodded. "He's been sitting on the beach for three days now. Around that headland." I indicated a rocky outcrop a few clicks away. I told the Major about the order to shoot the old man, and suggested maybe he could talk sense into Task Force HQ.

We banked low around the headland and I spotted the old chap. He was standing in the water, waves swirling around his feet. I noticed with satisfaction that he was wearing my bush hat. A flock of gulls took flight as we approached, swirled round, then settled farther along the beach. The old man glanced at us, then walked back to his crates and squatted. He removed his hat and tucked it in his trousers.

With the Major able to verify my story, I thought it was worth trying Task Force again. "Keep an eye on him," I called to the Major, then climbed the chopper so I could use the radio.

Once again I suggested it would be a good idea to send another chopper to pick the old guy up. Again I was told to wait. As I circled I spotted a Huey flying south about a mile inland. I could see from its tail markings it was an RAAF chopper so I tried raising it on my FM radio. There was no reply.

Task Force came back. "No aircraft available," the radio operator advised. I quickly explained I was watching an Australian Huey heading south. I knew he must be on the artillery warning net so I suggested they call him. The reply was immediate: "Negative!"

"Okay, then we'll pick him up," I replied. I was wary of the possibility that the VC were using the old guy as bait for an ambush, but if I was the VC I'd choose a better place. The jungle was patchy where it met the beach, in fact it was hardly jungle at all, just thin scrub dotted with scraggly casurina trees. I could see through the foliage easily and I couldn't spot any VC waiting to jump us.

We'd have to cram the old boy in the middle seat. He was nothing but skin and bone so the extra weight would be no problem. I could land on the damp sand above the water line — that way the rotor wash wouldn't kick up a storm — and I could keep an eye on the area just in case.

While I was pondering the problem, Task Force came up on the radio. "You will not pick him up!" a voice crackled as we dropped towards the beach.

"Say again?" I demanded.

"Do *not* pick him up." The voice was adamant.

"Then tell that Nine Squadron Huey to divert and get him," I complained. The RAAF Huey was now less than a mile away.

"That is uneconomical aircraft usage," came the reply.

I couldn't beleive my ears. Since when were they trying to run the war to a budget? "Then whistle up another, *economical* fucking aircraft — we'll keep an eye on him!" I was angry. Task Force was sounding like an accountant with a cost overrun.

"Stand by," Task Force replied tersely. I watched the Australian Huey dwindle towards Vung Tau. Maybe it was a Dust-Off taking wounded to the evac hospital. In that case a diversion wasn't justified. But knowing the way Nine Squadron operated it was more than likely they'd been out for a joy flight and the crew was dashing to Vung Tau for cocktails by the swimming pool.

The next transmission from Task Force took me by surprise. "Shoot him," the distant voice ordered.

I looked at my passenger. The Major's thumb was twitching near his M-16's safety catch. The radio crackled. "I say again, you will kill him, then get identification. Acknowledge!"

I didn't reply. I'd already decided that we'd pick him up. I dropped steeply towards the beach. The old man stood up as we spiralled down. He clasped his hands and bowed. We were at fifty feet when, without warning, the Major fired a long burst from his M-16. The rounds whipped the sand near the old man's feet. He didn't move, but stood rock still, hands under his chin. As the bullets chewed closer he bowed again.

"Christ! what the hell are you doing?" I yelled. The Major was leaning out of the cockpit, rifle to his shoulder. He pumped another burst at the old man. I banked hard left to throw his aim off, but I reacted too late. The bullets slashed across the old man's chest, flinging him back onto his crates. He slid onto the sand and lay staring at the sky.

I climbed the chopper then pulled around in a tight turn. "Why did you do that?" I screamed at the Major.

"Orders, Lieutenant," the Major replied. He coolly changed magazines and applied the safety.

Orders. The eternal excuse for everything around here — including murder. Suddenly I was beyond anger.

"I have to examine the body," the Major reminded me.

I checked to see whether we'd drawn attention from the treeline. Except for the twisted, wide-eyed corpse, the beach still looked like a page from a tourist brochure. The surf was alive with sparkling, well shaped waves. It would be a nice shore break — if I had the inclination to go surfing.

Reluctantly I dropped the chopper towards the bleeding sand.

Beware the enemy within . . .

NUI DAT

Gavin Bucknell was a Sergeant with the 3rd Battalion. He was a tall West Australian, thirty-two years old, a veteran of Malaya and Borneo. Bucknell had only recently arrived as a replacement for an NCO wounded soon after the battalion's arrival. This was his second tour of Vietnam, his first being in 1965 when he was shipped home after being wounded in a mortar attack only thirty days before his year in country was up. This time he was determined to make the full three hundred and sixty-five days.

That day was one of the most memorable of my life. I'd arrived a week before from Australia and walked into the middle of the TET offensive. My battalion had been deployed on operations near Ben Hoa and I found myself stuck with the rear echelon at Nui Dat. That wasn't so bad, I guess, but wandering around empty tent lines while the rest of your mates are in action tends to get you down, particularly when some of them don't come back.

I'd drawn duty sergeant for a three day stretch. Being duty sergeant involved a lot of moving around the area — inspections of the battalion lines, cookhouse, perimeter — all routine and very monotonous. However, there was an air of tension at Nui Dt because of the possiblity of an attack. So it was important to make sure our perimeter was manned effectively with what little manpower remained.

Because I was in and out of the battalion HQ most of the day and night I'd decided not to carry my 7.62mm SLR rifle, but opted to wear a nine millimeter pistol. Unlike a rifle it was convenient to carry around in its waist holster. Early that morning I was in the duty room. I'd finished inspecting the tent lines, then grabbed a mug of tea and a fist-full of biscuits from the cookhouse. Being a conscientious soldier I always cleaned my weapon every morning. So as I sat at my desk examining the morning reports, sipping tea and munching biscuits, I began cleaning my pistol.

I'd just stripped the weapon's magazine when the phone rang. It was Task Force HQ wanting our ration status. I searched the papers on the desk for my notebook, then realised my hands were full. I had a partly munched biscuit in one and a bullet in the other. In a moment of fumbling distraction I put the biscuit on the table, the bullet in my mouth, took a sip of tea and swallowed.

I realised what I'd done as I felt the cold metal lump slide down my throat. However, duty came first. I gave Task Force the information they needed, then rang off. I assembled my pistol, strapped it on, then headed for the Regimental Aid Post . . .

❖ ❖

The RAP was in a prefab steel hut beside battalion HQ. The Medical Officer was away with the rest of the battalion. In his absence the RAP was staffed by a corporal named Briggs and his assistant. Briggs had been a baker's apprentice prior to being drafted. He was short with red hair and a face crowded with freckles which merged whenever he smiled. The Army, for reasons best known to itself, trained him as a medical orderly. Surprisingly, Briggs was competent in his job; he knew the symptoms of most diseases and could detect a malingerer at fifty paces.

In the MO's absence, sick parade consisted of dispensing aspirins to the hung-over or prescribing anti-diarrheatics to the inevitable sufferers of Ho Chi Min's revenge. Anything serious Briggs referred to the Task Force HQ medical centre.

With the battalion out on operations, today's roll up had been small: a few booze-induced aching heads and one case of foot rot. As the last patient entered the dispensary, Briggs sighted the tall, menacing figure of Sergeant Bucknell lurking near the door. He didn't like Bucknell. The Sergeant had that acutely developed soldier's intuition that made it impossible for Briggs to fudge records, flick supplies or assign light duties to his mates. So Briggs dragged out the examination (a simple case of tinea) and let Bucknell fidget impatiently in the waiting room. After ten minutes of careful swabbing and tut-tutting he sent the patient on his way.

"Next!" Briggs called.

Bucknell waited until the departing patient was out of earshot before making his move. Briggs smirked. He'd been confidant to hundreds of soldiers suffering the early symptoms of lust-associated complaints contracted in the whorehouses of Vung Tau. Obviously this terror of the enlisted men was suffering from a similar affliction: officers and NCOs tried to keep their ailments confidential, especially problems below the waist.

Bucknell stepped into the dispensary and shot a withering stare at the assistant orderly, who took the hint and fled.

"Yes Sergeant, what seems to be the problem?" Briggs ventured in his best doctor-patient voice.

"I've swallowed a bullet," Bucknell blurted out.

Briggs had been expecting crutch rot or a drippy dick. The revelation caught him off guard. However, he maintained his composure. Briggs' clinical mind tried to visualise someone swallowing a 7.62mm round. They were big cartridges, the length of an index finger, with a pointed nose that would probably lodge in the gullet. He peered at Bucknell's throat for any signs of distension. Seeing none, he casually asked the only question that came to mind. "What calibre was this bullet?"

"Nine millimeter."

"Ah, that explains it," Briggs nodded sagely. A nine mill slug was short and rounded, like the end of a thumb. It would slide down easily. "Was it a *live* round?"

"Yes, it was a bloody live round!"

"And when did you swallow it?" Briggs fidgeted with a thermometer, resisting an impulse to take Bucknell's temperature.

"About five minutes ago."

"Have you tried throwing up?"

"Shit! Of course I have!" Bucknell was becoming agitated. 'I haven't had much to eat. I poked my fuckin' hand halfway down m'throat — no result!"

Briggs was stumped. Although he'd seen the MO deal with foreign object ingestion, they'd been the usual collection of trinkets; coins, safety-pins . . . one soldier even swallowed a St Christopher medal on a gold chain. But no one, to his knowledge, had ever swallowed a live bullet. The usual treatment for foreign objects was a harsh dose of laxative, then let nature take its course. The army's standard purgative was a fearsome brew which reacted in a fashion similar to a blazing Bengal curry. Briggs was reluctant to try this remedy: he knew that heat and live ammo didn't mix. The thought of the round cooking-off and Sergeant Bucknell splattering all over the RAP's neat white painted walls was repulsive. All he could think of asking next was: "Had anything to eat or drink since?"

"Look Briggs, don't just stand there bumpin' yer gums, do something." Bucknell poised his rigid index finger near the little Corporal's nose.

Briggs backed away and scratched his head. His Ben Casey

image was fading. "I need to know what's in your stomach — apart from the bullet."

"Half a mug of tea and a biscuit."

"Okay, I think maybe you should take a big drink of water."

"Water? Why, f'Christ sake?"

"To dilute the digestive juices. Your stomach's full of strong acid. It's probably eating into the cartridge primer —"

"The primer? Shit, you mean —"

Briggs realised this was an opportunity to strike back. He puffed out his freckled cheeks in a mock explosion.

Bucknell paled. "All right, where's something to drink?"

Briggs pointed at the dispensary refrigerator. "There's a jug of water in there. Meanwhile I'll consult with the Task Force MO and see what he suggests." He slipped from the room, leaving Bucknell fumbling in the fridge.

A few minutes later Briggs returned, his composure restored. Bucknell had drained the jug and was searching for more water. "What now?" he demanded.

"The Task Force MO says we should get you to the First Field Hospital at Vung Tau as quick as possible. They're checking to see if they can get an aircraft to fly you down. Meanwhile, you're to take it easy."

Bucknell sank into a canvas chair. He stared grimly at the dispensary wall. Among the medical charts were posters reminding soldiers against fraternising with the local women and the dangers of malaria. One was a re-creation of a World War Two propaganda banner with the shadowy Nazi threat substituted by leering Orientals. Bucknell broke out in a cold sweat. It read: *Beware the Enemy Within.*

In many ways the Army is like a big corporation. It uses an administrative system that caters for every aspect of a soldier's existence, from his need for food, to ammunition, even to ensuring he is given a decent burial. To some it may seem cumbersome; however, it must be remembered the system is designed to function under conditions of stress, so the reporting methods used are almost ritualised to minimise confusion. Each day a battalion will report to higher headquarters, among other items, its available manpower, its sick, and, after action, its casualties.

So, after Corporal Briggs completed his diagnosis of Bucknell's complaint, he diligently filed the appropriate paperwork. As the information threaded its way through the channels, like a message in a child's party game its context became subtly altered.

At 1100hrs, 161 Flight's Command Post received a request from Task Force HQ to fly an infantry Sergeant with a bullet in his stomach to Vung Tau. The standby helicopter was hastily fitted with a litter and the pilot briefed. A few minutes later it lifted off and headed for the 3rd Battalion's pad at the eastern end of the base.

It was 1105hrs when Corporal Briggs received a message from battalion HQ ordering him to prepare his casualty for litter transport. The fact that the system was now referring to Bucknell as a casualty didn't concern him: in a war zone anyone needing medical attention tended to be pigeon-holed in that all-embracing category.

Sergeant Bucknell was ordered to lie on a stretcher, found himself covered with a blanket, then whisked with great urgency to the chopper pad. He feared the worst. That freckle-faced imp Briggs was obviously keeping something from him. Bucknell was now convinced he was pregnant with explosives, a human time bomb with stomach acids eating away relentlessly towards the moment of birth. The very thought increased his nervousness, stimulating the acids he was trying desperately to suppress. By the time he arrived at the pad he was suffering acute heartburn. His thoughts became a web of fears. Which way was the bullet pointing? It it was up, it could shoot him in the brain, if down, it might blow his arse off.

"Jesus wept!" Bucknell groaned as the stretcher bearers hustled him beneath the slashing chopper blades and strapped him to the skids.

The helicopter's pilot was Ross Hutchinson:

"I landed at the pad and the casualty was waiting. As the medics secured him in the starboard litter I could see he was in pain. He grimaced and muttered something, but I couldn't hear over the clatter of the engine and rotors. I yelled to the little red-headed Corporal in charge, suggesting he accompany me to keep an eye on the patient.

The Corporal shook his head and indicated there was no need. He seemed absolutely confident the patient would survive the twenty-minute flight without attention. So I leaned forward, gave the brave soldier on the litter an encouraging smile, then waved everyone away. As soon as the medics were clear of the pad I wound on power and climbed slowly away.

As we cleared the trees and banked south towards Vung Tau, I took another glance at the patient. He was lying on his back, white-faced, watching me intently. I gave him a thumbs-up to boost his spirits. He smiled weakly at me.

God, they make these men tough, I thought. He's been gut-shot and he's not complaining."

"All personnel on R&R leave in Australia will refrain from the activity referred to as *Punch a Postie*. Disciplinary action will be taken against any personnel reported taking part in said activity."

Task Force Routine Orders

NUI DAT, 1200HRS

Ned Kelly

During the morning there'd been a constant barrage of demands from Task Force HQ for aircraft support. They were becoming increasingly nervous about enemy activity. Shoe-horning their requirements into the flight schedule hardly left us time to scratch.

A duty shift often lasted twelve to sixteen hours, with only an occasional break. This routine could drag on for weeks, depending on the intensity of enemy activity. Compared to the grunts in the jungle dodging bullets and booby traps, it was safe work. I always kept that in mind when I felt like complaining, but the relentless grind numbed the brain until you soon lost track of the days.

So, whenever there was a lull in activity, I took the opportunity to leave the CP and get some air. That day the pace had slackened by noon, so I decided it was time for a break. I tossed

Dave Brown for who'd go first. I won, and left him to fend off Queeg.

I squinted against the glare as I emerged into the sun. The air was hot and deathly still. There was a small knoll with a view across the airfield about fifty metres from the command post. I walked up the slope and sat on the grass in the dappled shade from the rubber trees. From here the Task Force looked deceptively peaceful. A heavy silence had come with the sun's zenith. Even the incessant drumming of helicopter rotors was missing; the only intrusion was the hollow crackle of detached voices drifting from our CP radios. At the end of the runway I could see our windsock, torn, faded and limp. I cursed our QM.

There'd been a brief rain shower a half hour ago. Although it was the dry season, squalls occasionally swept in from the coast and dumped rain in isolated areas. This one had cut across the western end of the base, filled the drainage ditch beside the runway, then headed west towards Saigon.

Three US Army Hueys were parked on the southern edge of the strip like tired green insects. Their doors were open and the crews were sprawled about on the cabin floor. The guns south of the runway were silent, their crews resting in the shade beneath tarpaulins strung over ammunition cases. It was almost as if a truce had been declared because it was too hot to fight.

To the west a sea of stunted brown grass stretched from the barbed wire to the jungle's edge about a kilometre away. It was cut by the remains of Highway Two, a crumbling track that briefly followed a smoothly tarred diversion around the end of the runway before resuming its bumpy path north. On it, two carts hauled by weary oxen with horns dragging the ground waded through the heat.

A dust-devil struggled into the sky from the area missed by the rain. It prowled the runway like a malevolent spirit. Halfway down the strip, dug into an area on the southern side, was the Task Force's rubbish dump. The twister fell among the smouldering refuse, siphoning newspapers into the sky. Suddenly it stopped, seemingly exhausted by the effort, leaving a tower of debris floating high in the air. Sheets of newspaper fluttered towards the jungle like giant butterflies. I wondered what the VC would make of *the Sydney Morning Herald*'s society pages.

A USAF forward air controller's Bird-Dog aircraft flew overhead and joined the circuit. I could see a kangaroo symbol on the aircraft's tail — the pilot was a lieutenant colonel, callsign Jade Zero Six. He was part of the USAF liaison group at Task Force HQ and often dropped into our CP for an update on the area.

Zero Six was a wiry little guy with a crew cut and a polite nature, the very antithesis of the stereotype cigar-chomping, pistol-packing American Eagle. He'd spent his share of time drinking with us at our mess and we found he was one of those types you couldn't help but like. He was the father of three children at college in California and he confided that this was probably his last flying posting before being sent home to a desk job. Prior to being a forward air controller, he'd flown almost every aircraft in the US Air Force's inventory, including B-52s. His stories of how hs squadron had been on airborne alert during the Cuban missile crisis with nukes cocked made us realise how close the world had come to all-out war. His primary target then, he said, was a Soviet submarine base near Murmansk on the Arctic circle. His B-52 had been armed with four twenty-megaton H-Bombs . . . roughly the equivalent of *four thousand* Hiroshima bombs. Now he flew a Bird-Dog armed with four seventeen-pound smoke rockets. "A come-down from eighty million tons of TNT," he admitted. "But a helluva lot more fun."

We suspected that Zero Six had a penchant for mischief that had resulted in his banishment to the wilderness of Vietnam rather than seeing out his time in the comfort of a SAC base. Recognising him as a soul brother, we made him an honorary Australian by "zapping" his aircraft with a kangaroo symbol on the rudder. He wore it with pride.

Jade Zero Six circled the airfield like a grey vulture, engine throttled back to a mutter as if he was afraid of disturbing the silence below. His aircraft lined up with the runway and slowed, the propeller a flickering silver disk as it floated towards the ground. The wheels touched with protesting squeals and the aircraft bounced, as if rejecting the scorching bitumen before gingerly plip-plopping back onto the runway. It trundled to the refuelling point and shut down. Zero Six climbed out, stretched, then walked to the side of the runway and took a leak. He rezipped, then chatted with the ground crew as they pumped fuel. No doubt he was also keeping an eye on them to ensure his aircraft didn't fall victim to their light-fingered ways.

I shut my eyes and leaned back against the trunk of a rubber tree. My thoughts wandered. I'd been in Vietnam almost six months. Another six and I could kiss the Army good-bye. I was a conscript. Before I'd won the lottery I'd been an advertising copywriter. My life had been a simple, nine-to-five routine during the week, followed by surfing and womanising over the weekend.

Oddly enough, I now felt little animosity towards the Army for its unwanted intrusion into my life. At first the Army had appeared as a faceless machine, notorious for bad food and loud-mouthed sergeants. However, when I discovered it wasn't possible to grasp the Army by the throat or kick it to death, I adopted the attitude that the only thing was to make the best of the next two years. Once the initial shock was absorbed, I found the Army began to take on a personality of its own. I'd learned that the Army was people, all of them with strengths, weaknesses, and personalities beneath their military facades. Some were predictably stereotyped, but others were outrageous nonconformists — many of whom, it seemed, were in 161 Recce Flight. A crazier bunch would be hard to find.

There were exceptions of course. The Army had its aberrations and I regarded Queeg as a prime example. Staying ahead of Queeg's machinations was becoming harder than fighting the VC. Although he was only one of a number of Task Force officers I dealt with daily, he was certainly the most unpleasant. I couldn't get a handle on the little bugger. Even our own commanding officer acknowledged that Queeg was a first-class prick. All I could do was to try not to let him get to me, as Dave Brown had suggested.

However, the place was starting to get on my nerves. The pounding of artillery, the clatter of choppers and the colour green haunted me daily. And I was learning that the Task Force wasn't quite the smoothly oiled fighting machine it was made out to be.

Apart from today's incidents, there were rumours about friction between the battalion COs and the Task Force commander: the Brigadier had become complacent, out of touch, the whisperings claimed. He'd been on leave during the start of the TET offensive, against the advice of senior staff who'd tipped the assault. Now, they said, like Westmoreland, he was trying to put on a Gung-Ho face.

There were tales of blistering arguments between the battalion commanders and the Brigadier, who wanted more enemy bodies to impress the politicians. The battalion commanders, to their credit, were resisting the temptation to emulate the Americans. They weren't going to risk their men for the sake of meaningless statistics. What mattered, they argued, was that despite TET, they'd prevented the VC from operating effectively in Phuoc Tuy Province. This allowed the local population to get on with the job of living; for the first time in years the rice harvest had been brought in without being taxed or destroyed by the VC and the roads remained open, allowing trade between villages to continue. That was what the Vietnam war was all about, they insisted — not creating mountains of dead to impress pork-barrelling politicians.

Such furphies made great bar talk, but even if they were unfounded they still left nagging doubts about why we were in Vietnam. Australian methods had proved successful so far and knocking senior officers had been a soldier's prerogative since Julius Caesar. But lately an air of frustration was starting to permeate Nui Dat. Small inconsistencies began to attract our attention. We'd noticed the newspapers flown in weekly weren't always in date sequence. The reason, we discovered, was that editions headlining anti-war demonstrations were being removed. This fumbling attempt at censorship by the Defence Department only made us suspicious of those in Australia who were supposedly looking after our interests. It was soon stopped — but what other information was being withheld and what lies were we being fed?

At home, demonstrations against the war were on the increase. Instead of being diggers carrying on the ANZAC tradition, we were labelled war criminals. The politicians who'd sent us were now standing on the sidelines, fingers in the wind.

Where they'd previously been only too willing to leap on their soap boxes and make rousing speeches in our support, now they were silent. Everyone seemed to be getting in on the anti-war act — the dock unions were refusing to load supplies, while other unions were raising funds to support North Vietnam. Although the supply embargoes were easily overcome by drawing on the American system, there were some items the Yanks couldn't provide. The most important of those was the mail. In a burst of anti-war sentiment, postal unions had black-banned mail to the Australian Task Force.

Mail from home was regarded as sacred. It was the one tangible link we had with friends and lovers. The fact that it was possible to hold a piece of paper that only days before had been written by someone who cared, was a boost to the spirit in a world where killing took priority. To deny us this was, in our minds, hitting way below the belt.

Some politicians were also encouraging people to write to soldiers and express their disapproval of the war. This led to a rash of poison-pen letters suggesting that wives and girlfriends were being unfaithful, some even giving names, dates and places. Dirt such as this we didn't need.

Like most other Nui Dat bachelors, I had a girl at home. I hadn't received a letter from her in more than a week. Although I suspected the delay was due to the union ban, it didn't stop the old jealousies and fears from parading themselves across my mind. I reached into my breast pockeet and took out a notebook. Pressed between the pages was her smiling photo. I looked at her until I ached, then snapped the book shut. Hopefully the mail would arrive today and I'd receive words from her reaffirming the faith. For all of us the dreaded *Dear John* letter was the ultimate disaster, second only to stepping on a mine.

No doubt this vignette was re-enacted many times among Australian soldiers. Everyone had their own way of dealing with it. But it was an uncertainty we could have done without. And because of it Australians died. Only two weeks ago, a friend in one of the infantry battalions had been torn apart by a landmine. They said he'd been worried by the last letter he'd received from his fiancee. He'd written back and was a jumble of nerves waiting for her reply. During a patrol he'd taken his eye off the ball just long enough to miss the telltale bamboo spike in the ground indicating there was a mine ahead. He died in the Dust-Off chopper on the way to the Evac hospital. The letter from his fiancee arrived a week later, postmarked a week before his death.

Australian unions were more unpopular with us than the VC. One prominent union leader had been drawn in caricature by a soldier artist. The lifelike sketch had been duplicated and took pride of place on dart boards throughout the Task Force. Some latrines even featured sheaves of these beetle-browed portraits for use as toilet paper. We joked that his face had wiped a thousand arses. While such behaviour might in retrospect seem puerile, the fact was our feelings ran deep. We were the ones facing the bullets, not the unions and certainly not their leaders. And it was *our* friends who were being maimed or killed with weapons the unions were helping to finance. And, as government politicians were either powerless or unwilling to break the union mail bans, we figured anything we could do to humiliate those involved was fair with us.

A breeze stirred the trees around me. It blew from the east and brought with it the faint, musty aroma of the South China Sea. I wondered what this country would be like without a war. The French had named the coastline to the east the Riviera of the Orient. I'd often flown over ruined mansions lining the beach; through their shattered walls lay ornate tiled floors and marble columns. Many had huge courtyards surrounded by frangipanni, bougainvillea and other tropical plants growing wild.

I'd come to the conclusion that Vietnam had once been a tropical paradise which had been fucked up by corrupt politicians and greedy colonial masters. I didn't quite know what category we came into.

The sound of an engine bursting into life snapped me back to reality. Jade Zero Six had finished refuelling and was taxiing to the end of the strip. The aircraft lined up, powered down the runway then climbed away. It banked south and disappeared over the rubber trees as one of our choppers flew in from the east. The war was starting up again.

As I walked back to our CP, I wondered if Jade Zero Six had problems with his mail.

Pedro Taylor

The flight back from the coast took only fifteen minutes. I pushed the chopper hard, skimming the jungle in an effort to scrub the bloody image of the old man from my mind. I was gripped by a sense of frustration and anger, but no matter how recklessly I flew, I could still see the old man standing there, calmly waiting to die.

As we banked round the tree tops, cartridge cases that had ejected into the forward cockpit bubble rolled about like scum in a ship's bilge. Each metallic clink was an echo of a bullet fired, a reminder of just how cheap death is. The Major's rifle was wedged between the seats and the stench of burned cordite seeped from the weapon. The old man wouldn't go away.

During the return flight I'd watched the Major examine the blood-smeared package he'd taken from the old man. His hands trembled as he unwrapped the pathetic brown oilskin. Inside was a leather wallet, a tobacco pouch and an old ivory pipe. I saw imprints around the pipe's bowl where, over the years, the old man's fingers had lovingly worn smooth the delicate carving.

The wallet contained documents which included a plastic-coated identification card. In one corner of the card was a passport photo. Below the wrinkled face, printed in Malay, Chinese and English, was the man's name, age and occupation. According to this, the old Chinese was the skipper of a junk trading between Singapore and Formosa. He was sixty-eight years of age. There was also a bundle of dog-eared photos in the wallet. The Major fanned them like a hot poker hand. I saw a family group. Children, cheerful faces — one was an elegant woman with a haunting smile, possibly the old man's wife. I could imagine him sitting on the gently moving deck of his creaking junk at sunset, smoking his pipe while lovingly poring over these precious reminders of home. The Major quickly tucked the photos away before the faces became judge and jury. He then unfolded a water-smeared document and held it flapping in the draughty cockpit.

It was a cargo manifest. Typed in English, it was date-stamped ten days ago in Singapore. It listed the junk's cargo as three hundred drums of cooking oil.

The Major's face paled as he read. "Cooking oil!" he whispered. He rewrapped the package and placed it on the seat between us.

I circled Nui Dat, noticing how peaceful the base appeared in the midday heat. Except for a departing USAF Bird Dog, the place seemed deserted. The smoke from the garbage dump was showing about five knots from the east. I turned into the wind and eased the helicopter onto our pad.

As I throttled down, the Major glanced at me. He nodded grimly, then, clutching his M-16, climbed slowly from the cockpit. He didn't speak; he merely stood in a half-crouch under the swooshing rotor blades, his eyes avoiding mine as he refastened his harness on the seat. His hands were shaking and he fumbled with the buckles.

I watched him walk away from the aircraft. He didn't look back. He'd have to live with the knowledge that in his eagerness to notch his gun, he'd killed an innocent man. The problem was, so would I.

Ned Kelly

If looks could kill, the expression on Pedro Taylor's face as he walked into the Command Post would have slayed legions. I prepared to dive for cover, but instead of throwing something, he went to the bench, took a blank recon report and wrote quickly.

"Get this to Task Force." He handed it to me.

I looked at the VR report. On it, was written in neat letters: "Today we killed an innocent man." I stared at Pedro. "What happened?" I asked.

He explained, then held out a brown oilskin package. "This was his."

I took it, peered inside and saw the old man's identity card. "Christ almighty," I whispered.

Dave Brown walked across the CP and stood beside me. I passed the package to him. He unwrapped it, examined the photos and pipe. "The Major shot him?" he asked.

Pedro nodded.

"But why?" I demanded.

"Who knows," Pedro shrugged.

Gingerly Dave refastened the bundle and put it on the bench. "I'll get this over to Task Force," he said. — "Oh shit!" he suddenly swore, staring at his hands. They were smeared with blood. I looked at mine; they too were bloody. Pedro held up his palms. They were red. We all looked at the old man's tobacco pouch.

From it oozed a little crimson pool. It was a very bad omen.

NUI DAT, 1430HRS

Ned Kelly

I tried to put the old man's death out of my mind by telling myself this was a war and such things happened. But it only raised questions that I couldn't answer. Almost twenty five years later, they still remain unanswered. I didn't know it then, but that wasn't the end of the incident. We felt a strong sense of responsibility for the old man — we had found him, and we had unwittingly brought about his death. For the next two weeks our first and last light recons flew over the old man's corpse. We watched his body bloat, then be picked clean by crabs and gulls. We made a point of daily requesting Task Force HQ to give him a decent burial; we were ignored. To them, it was as if the old man had never existed.

When I read stories of how Australians in Vietnam always respected enemy dead and took great care to ensure they were treated with reverence, I cast my mind back to that old man. There is no doubt an effort *was* made to treat enemy dead respectfully, and it's true that in most cases, wherever possible, they were buried with due ceremony. But the old man didn't fall into the category of enemy. In the eyes of the powers at Task Force HQ he was a nobody — a non-person. As such, he couldn't threaten careers or command ten seconds of television news time. And, if Task Force *had* decided to bury him, someone might be admitting a mistake. As it was, the moment the bullets struck, he ceased to exist both as a person and as a minor tactical problem. He became a sad casualty of war.

I know now it was the events of that morning that changed my attitude to the war. I didn't suddenly sprout long hair and hippy beads, or beat my rifle into a cabbage hoe. The VC and NVA were still out there committing atrocities against the South Vietnamese that made the old man's death pale by comparison. But it showed that we, the Australians, we Anzacs who prized a sense of fair play, mateship and common decency, were also capable of callousness of the highest order. We were *fallible*, just like the rest of the human race.

Fortunately, that afternoon I was too busy to dwell on the subject. Events were snowballing. Reports were coming in to Task Force HQ of enemy sightings. Most were from ARVN outposts jittery at the prospect of a VC attack during the coming night. It was our job to check them out.

Air recon could only do so much — one drawback was that aircraft were noisy and usually gave the enemy time to conceal themselves. The most effective means of deterring an enemy from infiltrating within striking distance of any base was for infantry to actively patrol the area. By doing this the enemy soon learned they stood a good chance of bumping into a patrol or being ambushed whenever they came near an outpost or base.

It was a tactic the Australian Army had proved time and again, and an example of how our methods differed greatly from the Americans. It was also one the ARVN were reluctant to implement. They tended to revert to the Americans' way of operating, relying on firepower, air recon, anything to avoid having to step foot in the dreaded jungle. I understood how they felt.

After their midday siesta, many ARVN outposts came to life. Some would dispatch squads that sprinted across the cleared ground in front of their bunkers, then dashed through the jungle's fringe before darting back to safety in a comic parody of a clearing patrol. Others would erupt like miniature volcanoes and send waves of machine-gun fire out into the jungle, followed by mortars, artillery — anything that made a noise. *Recon by Fire* was the buzzword the Americans used — they were the masters of the technique. Like kids whistling in a graveyard, all this did was make them feel better. It also consumed ammunition that was needed when an attack did come.

With the ARVN's imagination being spurred by the TET offensive, Task Force was having difficulty in sorting out who was genuine and who was crying wolf. We had one chopper and one fixed-wing on recon and as Queeg passed us the information we relayed it to whatever aircraft was closest to the alleged sightings. It was mayhem. The ARVN posts were bidding against each other and continually upping the stakes. VC squads had become platoons, platoons companies and companies, battalions. Theoretically some map squares were so crowded with VC there wasn't room for the trees. Our aircraft had checked out a dozen reports and drawn blanks on all of them. Then, at about 1500hrs, one of our Cessnas returning from a recon along the coast reported a sighting: two Viet Cong flags in trees near a road east of Nui Dat. He was low on fuel and couldn't check it out, so we passed the information to one of our choppers on reconnaissance nearby . . .

Lieutenant Roger Colclough

We were about five clicks east of the sighting when our CP radioed us the information, so I headed straight for the area. We flew low over route 328 until we came to a large section of dry rice paddys. There, atop a lone clump of trees in the middle of one of the fields, fluttered two VC flags. The yellow stars on their red-and-blue background stuck out like a dog's balls against the sky. It was a bold thumbing of the nose by the VC — I knew the flags hadn't been there during my first recon early in the morning. The local rice workers would have seen the culprits, but none of them were in the fields — they'd cleared out early. That was an ominous sign.

Already the radio call from our command post had alerted a USAF FAC, who arrived a few minutes before us. I recognised the aircraft: it was our old mate, Jade Zero Six. He was circling low over the trees like a hungry buzzard. I saw his aircraft slow as the flaps were lowered, then, on the verge of a stall, make a low pass over the flags. I wondered what the hell he was up to.

"Jesus, look at him!" my observer, Private Moore yelled. "The bugger's trying to snatch our flags!"

I stared at the Bird Dog. Trailing from the rear cockpit was a line attacked to a grappling hook!

"The bastard!" I swore, suddenly outraged that a Yank was going to steal our trophies. I gunned the throttle and pushed the chopper towards the flags. Zero Six saw me, then dropped in on my tail. Although slower, I had about two hundred metres start.

As we approached the first flag I told Moore to check out the top of the tree. I was wary: it looked like a set-up to me.

"Nothing, sir!" Private Moore insisted as we neared the flag. He was leaning out of the door, peering into the trees. The rotor wash thrashed at the branches, sending leaves swirling into the cockpit.

"You sure?" It sounded too good to be true. Surely the VC weren't going to waste two perfectly good flags.

"Yessir, this one's tied to the branches." Moore reached out as we drifted by.

I hope it's not tied too securely, I thought as he seized it. We were travelling at about ten knots. For a moment it looked as if he'd either lose an arm or be dragged from his seat harness as he hung on with a determined grip. But the flag pulled free and he hauled it aboard. He held it up. This wasn't some patchwork rag run up in a jungle tailor's shop. It was made from pure silk, beautifully woven and stitched. It had to be a Ho Chi Min original, made in North Vietnam.

"Okay, sir, that's one for you," Moore grinned as he bundled the flag and stuffed it at his feet. "Now let's get mine!" He pointed to the second flag.

I'd already decided we'd pushed our luck far enough. One flag was enough. I opened the throttle as we headed towards the second flag about twenty metres away. I knew we were going too fast for Moore to be able to snatch it, but to keep him happy I told him to check the tree-top, as if I intended turning for another pass.

"It's clear!" he called as we whipped past the fluttering silk.

At that instant everything turned red. The chopper felt as if it had been struck from beneath by a giant sledge-hammer. We were thrown forward and up. There were clanging sounds like gravel on a tin roof. The tree had been mined! Fortunately the engine behind us took the force of the blast — otherwise I'm sure we would have been shredded as fragments ripped through the aircraft.

My immediate reaction was to get the hell out of the place. Surprisingly, the engine still responded. I nudged the rudder pedals and turned away, but as I did so I heard Jade Zero Six call over the radio: "Better put it down, son. You're on fire."

Because he said it so calmly, yet with such fatherly authority I didn't ask questions. I headed for the road, but as I lined up, the engine quit. I auto-rotated, pulled pitch and flared a few feet above the ground. As we lost speed I *knew* Zero Six wasn't bullshitting; flames that had been forced back by the slipstream now blew forward and wrapped around the cockpit.

We skidded to a halt, scrambled out and ran for our lives — we wanted to put as much distance between us and the aircraft as possible. In the cockpit I carried white phosphorous grenades and they'd cook off any second.

We'd gone about fifty metres when warning bells sounded in my brain. "Landmines!" I shouted. We both went up on our toes like fire-walkers on a bed of glowing coals. I couldn't see any landmines, but the imagination works against you in these situations: in this country the next step could be your last. So we hot-footed it to the edge of the road and took a flying leap towards a drainage ditch. While in mid-air another bell clanged: "Pungi stakes!"

By sheer effort of will we defied gravity to convert a headlong dive into a feet-first landing. Fortunately there were no pungi stakes waiting to impale us; just hard, dry clay. We scrambled into the ditch and took cover.

Private Moore was carrying the M-60. He set it up and aimed

24 October 1967. 2nd Lt Weaver completes 365 days in Vietnam. **Back row, from left:** Captain Phil Roberts (2IC), 2nd Lt Adam Fritsch, author, Major George Constable (OC), 2nd Lt Mike Meehan, Lt Kev Peacock, 2nd Lt Blair "Bambi" Weaver, Captain Peter Robinson. **Middle row:** 2nd Lt Ross Goldspink, 2nd Lt Tom "The King" Guivarra, 2nd Lt Dave McFerran, Captain Bernie Forrest, Captain John Coggan. **Front:** Lt Ross Hutchinson, 2nd Lt Peter Garton. (Source: Denis Gibbons)

161 flight line. Cessna 180 facing. On right an O-1 Bird Dog, obtained by dubious means from the American Army. It was in this aircraft on 23 May 1968, that 161 Flight's OC, Major George Constable, was shot down and killed. Another Bird Dog was smuggled back to Australia in pieces by 161 members and now resides at the Museum of Army Flying at Oakey, Queensland. (Source: B. Forrest)

View from knoll outside 161's command post (Source: B. Forrest)

161 Sioux beside Luscombe Airfield. SAS hill in immediate background with Nui Thi Vi mountains in far distance. (Source: B. Forrest)

Mess hut. Tin roof and open sides. Always a welcome sight when returning from operations. (Source: B. Forrest)

Home among the rubber trees. Each tent held two and was improved by successive occupants. Most important were the sand-bagged walls to protect from mortar fragments. (Source: B. Forrest)

Remains of Roger Colclough's barbequed Sioux (Source: O.M. Eather)

Roger Colclough (second from left) celebrating his lucky escape after the episode with the VC flags (Source: B. Forrest)

17 December 1967. Christmas party among the rubber trees. (Source: O.M. Eather)

Lieutenant Glen Duus during a twenty-four hour stint as duty officer (Source: B. Forrest)

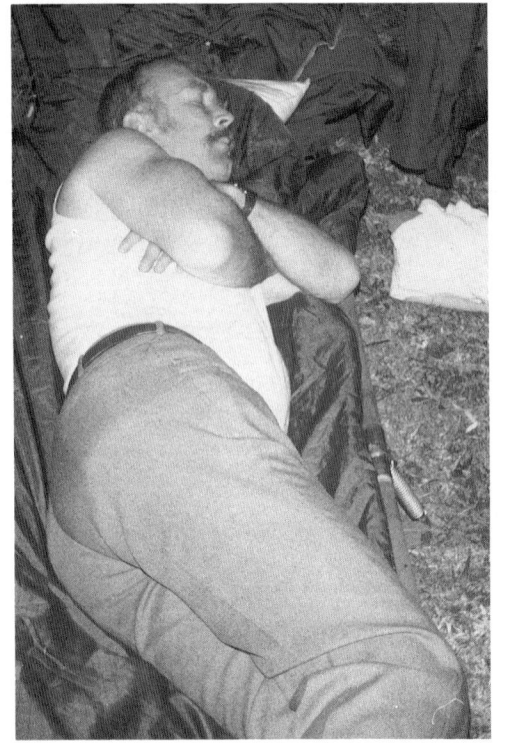

Lieutenant Glen Duus resting on Sioux litter between sorties. Location was beach near Cape Ho Tram during operations in October 1967. (Source: O.M. Eather)

Rip Van Winkle? Glen Duus (now Lt Colonel, retired) photographed almost a quarter of a century later at a 161 Flight reunion. Legend has it he was bitten by a Tsetse Fly early in his Vietnam tour. (Source: B. Forrest)

Route 328 viewed from 161 Cessna on recon (Source: O.M. Eather)

USAF Forward Air Controller's Bird Dog operating out of Nui Dat. This may have been Jade Zero Six's aircraft. (Source: B. Forrest)

Vietnamese girls selling fruit to soldiers on leave at Vung Tau beach (Source: B. Forrest)

Concert at Nui Dat's Luscombe Bowl by Aussie entertainers, Christmas 1967. The efforts of performers including Pattie McGrath, Lorrae Desmond, Col Joy and Denise (Ding Dong) Drysdale were always appreciated by the residents of Nui Dat. (Source: B. Forrest)

it down the road. I looked back at the chopper — it was burning to a crisp. The WP grenades cooked off with muffled bangs, sending white trails arcing gracefully into the sky. I remember thinking: *That's just cost the tax payers a hundred grand!*

"VC!" Private Moore yelled.

I turned to see an ox cart about two hundred metres away. It had rounded a corner of the road and was lumbering towards us. Sitting on the cart, spurring the plodding animal with a bamboo pole, was a sleepy Vietnamese peasant wearing a conical straw hat. He pushed on, head down, oblivious to the drama ahead of him.

Moore was convinced we were facing a VC cavalry charge. He cranked a round into the M-60s breech and before I could say Ho Chi Min, opened up. Fortunately for the driver, Moore's aim was bad.

Inspired by the hail of bullets crackling over his head, the driver sprang to life. He wheeled the creaking cart around and took off like Ben Hur. The ancient wagon obviously wasn't built for speed; it had only gone about fifty metres when both wheels popped off and bounced away into the paddy field. The driver remained standing on the skidding tray, cracking his whip over his head at the pounding oxen. He disappeared around the corner in a cloud of dust, pursued by wild streams of tracer.

I looked at Moore, remembering my training on the M-60: controlled bursts of five to ten rounds, said the book. Moore was doing anything but. His finger was glued to the trigger in what looked like an attempt to fire the longest sustained burst ever achieved with the weapon. The gun's deafening *buda-buda-buda* made it impossible to talk. The ammo belt was disappearing like a snake down a rabbit hole while cartridge cases were piling in a glistening mound on the other side. Moore himself was vanishing inside a cloud of smoke and dust. Finally all I could see was a swirling blue cordite haze with a pair of boots sticking out one end and a red hot barrel out the other.

The last tracer flickered into the sky and the bolt clunked on an empty chamber. As the smoke cloud drifted away, Moore eased the sizzling gun from his shoulder. He looked at me with satisfaction.

I had to admit he'd frightened the VC cavalry away very effectively. But he'd used all our ammunition *and* missed the target — quite a remarkable feat seeing he'd fired almost a hundred rounds at the poor bugger. Anyway, it seemed we weren't going to have to make a stand of it — Jade Zero Six had called for help and it was already starting to arrive.

Jade Zero Six

Last thing I wanted to see was an Aussie casualty. So as the chopper dropped toward the road I put out a call on my TAC AIR frequency: *Aussie pilot down!* The replies were immediate. You guys had established such a gutsy reputation that we considered it a privilege to be able to help. In fact, because I'd called on TAC AIR frequency, aircraft from all over Vietnam were coming up and offering assistance. I think I could've redirected the entire US air effort into Phuoc Tuy Province within five minutes. If I'd wanted a B-52 strike, I could've got it.

I saw the two crewmen clear the burning chopper and make it to a ditch beside the road. When one of them opened up with his M-60 I knew they were in trouble. So I called again: *Aussies under attack, get your asses here fast!*

To Roger Colclough it looked as if the entire US Air Force *was* arriving: First in was a Heavy Fire Team — three Huey gunships. They clattered over the rice field and immediately set about laying suppressing fire along the jungle fringe. They pumped the jungle full of bullets and explosive, using mini-guns, rockets and 40mm grenade launchers. The noise was deafening. They'd only been at it a few minutes when another Heavy Fire Team wheeled in and joined them. That made six gunships blazing away as if they'd found Ho Chi Min himself. Then, in the middle of this, four F-100s dropped down to join the party. Each carried about the same bomb load as a World War Two B-17. They quickly started adding napalm and bombs to the show. I thought, *Shit, there must be an NVA regiment coming after us!*

We were terrified, but simultaneously fascinated by the fireworks display. I saw more aircraft forming an orderly "cab rank" high overhead, tracing lazy patterns in the sky as they waited their turn to be called down by the FAC.

One thing the Americans know how to do well is use air power. In a few minutes I could see order forming among the chaos. The two Heavy Fire Teams were working the jungle fringe east, while the F-100s blasted it west of our position. We were in the middle of a zone protected by parallel walls of explosive. Jade Zero Six circled overhead, marking the target with smoke rockets, issuing directions, while nimbly avoiding the big jets as they streaked in, dropped their loads, then powered away using afterburner.

Down the middle of this aerial rodeo bored a US Army Dust-Off Huey. It skimmed the rice field then flared on the road beside us like a check-reigned stallion. As the skids bumped the ground, a huge hairy arm reached out, seized me by the shirt and dragged me aboard. Private Moore was likewise plucked up and dumped beside me. The chopper lifted off and headed for Nui Dat. I later learned we'd been on the ground less than five minutes.

Ned Kelly

We heard the action over our flight net. A small crowd had gathered around the PRC-25, reminding me of Saturday afternoon at the racetrack as we egged Roger on in his contest with Jade Zero Six. To us it sounded as if what started out as a minor incident had escalated into a major battle.

For a painful moment we thought Roger and his observer had bought it, but after a few minutes the rescue chopper came up on our frequency and announced both were okay. Private Moore had taken a shrapnel wound to his foot, but was otherwise fine. We breathed a collective sigh of relief.

I spoke with Jade Zero Six on our flight net and we soon pieced together what had happened. The second flag had been placed near an explosive charge concealed in the top of the tree. When Roger passed over it, his rotor wash tripped a device that detonated the charge. It seems this contrivance was intended to catch an aircraft — it certainly wouldn't have worked against anything else. We grudgingly admitted it, the VC were bloody resourceful. At first we were reluctant to use the words "booby trap", however we later agreed it was the cunningest booby trap we'd ever heard of and credited Charley with one helicopter on the command post scoreboard.

Fortunately it was the only time we lost an aircraft this way. A few weeks later, there were reports of flags temptingly fluttering from trees in other provinces, but we never heard of anyone falling for it again. Bad news spreads fast.

Roger's charred Sioux was recovered by Chinook and slung back to the airfield later that afternoon. It was a write-off. The airframe had taken so many sharpnel hits it looked as if it had been attacked by white ants. Both fuel tanks had fist-sized holes punched through them, allowing avgas to drench the engine.

Roger and his observer had been lucky. If they'd been travelling more slowly the explosion would have been in front of the chopper. With only a plastic bubble to shield them, both men would've been mincemeat. They were also fortunate to have Jade Zero Six around to call in help quickly — even if his antics had prompted Roger to stretch his luck too far. The irony of it all was that the flag they'd captured was left in the cockpit in their hurry to escape.

So now we were two aircraft short. I shuddered at the thought of having to advise Queeg. Even though I knew he was aware of the fact that we'd lost an aircraft — they'd monitored part of the action on the Task Force HQ radios — they hadn't monitored our flight net. So I decided it was best to leave out the fact that Roger and Jade Zero Six had been competing for the flags when it happened. With a little imagination I could rearrange the truth to make the official report read like a combat citation. In the meantime I decided to phone Queeg and paper over the cracks under the pretext that our engineering officer needed to examine the aircraft before we could determine conclusively what brought the chopper down. I was learning to match Queeg at his own game.

When I phoned, Queeg wasn't in. One of his staff advised he

was off sulking somewhere. (Queeg was as unpopular with his staff as he was with us.) The Sergeant confided that his boss had his nose put out by the entire incident. It seemed Queeg had been looking forward to playing the role of rescue co-ordinator-cum-hero, but Jade Zero Six's prompt reaction had stolen his thunder.

Shush Mission

While Roger Colclough was collecting souvenirs east of the Task Force, about thirty clicks north of Nui Dat, a 161 Recce Flight Cessna 180 was conducting a recon of a different type. This aircraft was fitted with radio direction-finding equipment and carried a Signal Corps operator in its cramped rear seat. The equipment was developed by the Australian Signal Corps and was shoe-horned into the Cessna's tiny cabin with only one modification to the aircraft's external appearance: a small, saucer-shaped antennae slung beneath the wheel struts. From a distance it looked like a spare tyre and when the aircraft was flying it was hardly noticeable.

The aircraft was one of the Australian Task Force's most closely guarded secrets. The aircraft's function was Signals Intelligence (SIGINT) — locating enemy units by listening for their radio transmissions. The unit responsible for operating the equipment was 547 Signals Troop, a small band of electronics specialists who ran a mad professor's workshop tucked away in Task Force HQ. The men of 547 Sig Troop kept very much to themselves, a sure sign they'd been dubbed by the *Top Secret* sceptre. Accordingly their activities were only talked about in clandestine whispers, and their sorties became known as "Shush Missions".

161 Recce Flight had one fixed-wing aircraft permanently allocated for these missions. It flew each day, sometimes three or four sorties, such was the importance placed on the information gathered. The *Shush* aircraft would take off and cruise around at about five thousand feet while the operator scanned known enemy frequencies. Once a transmission was heard, a simple triangulation technique was used to plot its source. Although the

Australian equipment was relatively unsophisticated, it could trace a radio signal to within a kilometre — in contrast to the Americans, who used large aircraft festooned with antennae and crammed with the latest high-tech gear. However, the Americans found their accuracy was only about five kilometres, due mainly to the fact that they turned their aircraft towards the transmitter's location then flew towards it, immediately revealing the aircraft's purpose.

The VC, of course, had soon wised up to this practice. It didn't take them long to link the appearance of a flying porcupine with the arrival of a swarm of ground-attack aircraft. They quickly developed counter techniques, including posting sentries to warn of approaching aircraft, then shutting down and starting up a decoy transmitter a few kilometres away. It was an example of the fox outsmarting the hounds.

The Australian aircraft, on the other hand, apart from looking like one of the normal recon aircraft based at Nui Dat, didn't make a sudden about-face when a transmission was heard. This wolf-in-sheep's clothing would stay on course while rotating its concealed directional antennae to take bearings which were plotted on the map to reveal the transmitter's location.

This afternoon, the Australian operator had tuned into an enemy transmission and traced the signal to an area about thirty kilometres north-east of Nui Dat. The VC continued transmitting unaware that ten kilometres away, 161's inconspicuous little Cessna was skirting around the area, making its triangulation runs.

On landing, the information was taken direct to the G2 Intelligence at Task Force HQ. There the bearings were drawn again — this time the plot gave the position with an accuracy of less than four hundred metres. The tape recordings of the enemy transmissions were run and checked against a library of known enemy radio operators. In a few minutes a positive ID had been made. The enemy radio operator had been recorded before: his high speed and distinctive Morse "fist" identified him even though his transmissions were in code.

The G2 Int and his staff were cautiously excited. Because this particular enemy operator was exceptionally skilled he was a marked man and hence easy to track. American SIGINT aircraft had originally detected him almost two months ago, north of the DMZ. He belonged to the Headquarters of a North Vietnamese Regiment that was filtering down the Ho-Chi-Min trail via Laos and Cambodia. US SIGINT aircraft had tracked the regiment south but lost contact when the unit reached Cambodia. However, they knew the operator would resurface after his unit left their Cambodian sanctuary and crossed into South Vietnam. All SIGINT units (including the Australians) were warned to be on the lookout and were issued with sample tapes of the man's code style. Now he'd been found in Phuoc Tuy Province — and along with him, it was assumed, the NVA Regiment.

For Task Force Intelligence, this was another piece of a giant jigsaw puzzle. Occasionally Int staff had to hammer a little when fitting the pieces together but this one dropped neatly into place. The area where the radio operator was located had been under surveillance for several months. Aerial reconnaissance by 161 Recce Flight had first detected signs of occupation in the thick jungle thirty clicks north east of Nui Dat, marking it as a possible base camp. They'd kept it under light surveillance until a SAS patrol could be scheduled to investigate the area.

SAS had subsequently confirmed that local VC units were preparing what looked like a large base complex, including extensive underground installations. The four man patrol had kept the camp under surveillance, all but sitting in the enemy's lap while they observed the VC at work. SAS scouted the perimeter of the camp, estimated its dimensions, then were extracted without being detected.

The camp remained under observation. The area was declared off limits to intensive aerial surveillance: only a few apparently random over-flights by recon aircraft were permitted. This ruse was intended to reassure the enemy that their hideaway had not been compromised; too little or too much aircraft activity might arouse their suspicions.

From the avalanche of half-truths, rumours and lies that were filtered daily by Task Force Intelligence, more evidence was gathered. A picture started forming. Local VC units had been instructed to assign manpower to act as guides for a large main force unit. At first it was believed to be for the purpose of guiding a NVA battalion to join the battle in the Saigon/Ben Hoa area; however, there were indications that the unit was entering Phuoc Tuy Province in groups of fifty to one hundred. There were also signs of significant logistics activity to support the operation; supplies were being landed at night by sampan on the beach immediately east of the area.

One Intelligence source suggested that the enemy unit would rest after its long march down the Ho Chi Min trail at a specially prepared base camp somewhere North of Nui Dat. At first this was discredited, but the discovery of a new base area under construction fitted the theory.

Now the key to the jigsaw puzzle had been found. The radio operator identified by 161's SIGINT aircraft belonged to the headquarters group of the same NVA regiment. So it was a fair guess the regiment was now moving into its temporary base camp. But was the NVA Regiment there now or was the HQ group merely an advance guard? There was no way of knowing. The safest assumption to work on was that they were already at full strength, and a move towards Nui Dat could be expected at any time.

Task Force Intelligence realised the NVA's presence presented both a threat and an opportunity. The threat was obvious. To defend the Nui Dat base from such a force — estimated at over two thousand, plus reserves drawn from the local battalions which could add another two to four thousand — might require pulling back the two battalions now supporting the Americans' Ben Hoa operation. That would leave a hole in the defences that would dilute the American effort. And pulling two battalions out of Ben Hoa, then flying them back to Nui Dat would hardly go unnoticed. The helicopter lift would be observed by the VC, and their Int network would soon put two and two together. Within a matter of hours the NVA would be alerted and they'd bug out, then fade into the jungle.

On the other hand, attacking the area was out of the question. Against well dug-in positions, in thick jungle, the casualty rate would be horrific. Without accurate knowledge of what the enemy's actual strength was it could be downright suicide.

That left three options. The first was to draw the enemy out and hit him in an area where the odds were in the Australians' favour. Once again, to do that required withdrawing manpower from the Ben Hoa operation. On paper such a plan looked fine, encompassing classical military tactics: sweeping pincer movements and cut-off groups could be positioned to trap the enemy in any one of a number of killing fields.

However, the big stumbling block would be getting the enemy's co-operation. Expecting them to fall into the appointed killing ground on schedule was asking too much of an intelligent and resourceful enemy. As the French and, later, the Americans had painfully learned, the opposition wasn't that gullible.

The second option was to defend Nui Dat relying on artillery and American airpower to support the thinned defences. Preparations for this could be implemented immediately.

The final option was to target the enemy base camp for an airstrike. Its location was known and the NVA were either there now or moving in. If the strike was accurate there was a good chance of catching them. That was the problem. According to the SAS report the camp was large — possibly extending on top and beneath an entire map square. There was only one way of dealing with such an extensive target: a B-52 strike. Six aircraft each carrying seventy thousand pounds of bombs.

The G2 Int took the information to Senior Task Force Staff. It was decided that the opportunity to hit the camp with an airstrike was too good to miss. However, its success would rely on absolute secrecy; all too often warning of such strikes had leaked to the enemy. So a briefing outlining the situation was prepared for personal delivery by a senior Staff Officer to MACV HQ Saigon.

Meanwhile, the G2 Int was to prepare a briefing for all Task Force units, stressing the possibility of an attack on Nui Dat by a NVA force. No mention of the location of the enemy base camp or the probability of a B-52 strike was to be revealed at the briefing. Although security within the Task Force was tight and there was no contact with the local Vietnamese population, the commander was taking no chances. Only those senior officers and units who needed to know would be briefed on the full situation at a later time.

A message went out to all units at Nui Dat ordering commanders or their deputies to report to Task Force HQ for an urgent briefing.

TAN SON NHUT, 1500HRS

Mike Dawson

The comic opera reception committee had been performing flat out all day. So had the freight loaders. There was something spooky about a brass band tootling *Yankee Doodle* while the living entered stage right and the dead departed stage left. By mid-afternoon, when the aircraft flying us to Nui Dat finally arrived, we were happy to put Saigon behind us.

The RAAF Caribou clattered towards us and squealed to a halt with both engines churning, looking like an impatient green moose as it rocked to and fro on its landing gear. We stumbled through the prop wash to the tail ramp, clutching our gear as the loadmaster sergeant yelled for *us* to get the lead out. Blimpy stood nearby, engrossed in his clipboard, obviously relieved we were off his hands.

We climbed aboard and strapped into the hard webbed seats lining each side of the fuselage. In the middle of the hold was a pile of mail sacks secured by a cargo net. The loadmaster prowled up and down like a territorial animal, checking our harness and making sure our gear was stowed correctly. Satisfied all was secure, he spoke into his headset, gave us a thumbs up and closed the ramp.

As the square of light vanished, the airflow to the cargo bay stopped. It was an oven, reeking of petrol and vomit. As the Caribou lurched towards the runway the exhaust gases from both engines seeped into the hold. By the time we took off I was feeling queasy. I closed my eyes and leaned back against the vibrating fuselage. I couldn't help dwelling on the fact that less than twenty-four hours ago I'd been in Sydney, sitting at a hotel by the beach, drinking beer and eyeing the girls. Now I was flying over a foreign country in a clattering tin can, to some

Godforsaken place where people killed each other for a living. The entire concept was suddenly illogically obscene.

The whine of the cargo ramp opening attracted my attention. The loadmaster had noticed our uneasiness and the open ramp created a strong draught of fresh air through the hold. I guess he was tired of travelling with puking grunts — and even more tired of mopping up after them. I tempered my animosity towards him just a little.

I was getting my first close look at the country. We'd levelled at about five thousand feet, supposedly out of range of any VC who might take pot shots at us. It was a common occurrence, the loadmaster shouted. He pointed to a riveted plate on the side of the fuselage which he said was the result of ground fire.

I glanced out of the window. A patchwork quilt of rice paddys drifted beneath us, looking much like the wheatfields back home. Then I noticed they were pockmarked with craters. Some areas had craters within craters, where shells or bombs had lobbed in a tight pattern. I wondered what had prompted the use of such firepower, believing what I was seeing must be the aftermath of a major battle.

The rice fields gave way to jungle. It was thick, green, seemingly impenetrable, but it too was peppered with craters. I then realised the entire country was covered with bomb craters. Vietnam looked like the surface of the moon, the only difference being that Vietnam had more craters.

We flew over an area where the jungle had been flattened as if a giant foot had descended from the sky. The earth at the centre was ploughed in a scar five hundred metres wide for almost a kilometre.

"B-52 strike," the loadmaster called. "Four aircraft each carrying seventy thousand pounds of bombs."

I made a quick calculation. The weight of explosives dropped on that one patch of jungle was equivalent to a raid by fifty World War Two B-17s.

Suddenly we were over an area where the trees were glistening white skeletons standing above stunted foliage. "Defoliants," the crew chief answered the question on our faces. That was my introduction to the effects of *Agent Orange*. Twenty years later I'd still be seeing the tragic results of its use.

The forest of dead trees trailed behind us, stretching from horizon to horizon like an ancient graveyard. We flew into a rain squall, the rain drumming briefly on the fuselage before we emerged into bright sunshine. After another ten minutes the jungle petered out to more rice fields and their ubiquitous craters. We dropped lower and droned over a village. About twenty thatched bamboo huts stood in a clearing; some were burned out skeletons. Others looked near to collapsing. A few skinny oxen grazed in a field nearby.

Farther on was another, larger village beside a narrow stream. These houses were timber framed with flat corrugated iron roofs. All were laid out in neat rows on equal sized plots of ground. I later learned this was a village that had been resettled, the population moved from a VC area to one controlled by the Australian Task Force.

The aircraft banked hard left. We were over Nui Dat. I could see the runway's black scar dividing endless rows of rubber trees. South of the strip, a long feather of white smoke drifted from what I thought was a huge crater. I didn't realise it was the rubbish tip. My home for the next three hundred and sixty-five days looked very forbidding.

NUI DAT, 1600HRS

Ned Kelly

The jungle drums were beating. That potent brew of soldier's intuition and the wind in the rubber trees whispered that tonight was *the night*. The Bad Guys were massing out in the jungle like hostile Zulus. I could feel their beady eyes peering at us from the jungle fringe. They were going to slaughter us and make lampshades from our skins, shrink our heads, play billiards with our nuts . . .

It didn't pay to have an overactive imagination. Still, there *was* a feeling in the air like electricity before a thunderstorm when something big was about to happen. That afternoon my hair was virtually standing on end. All day the pin sticking and grease pencil marks cluttering our maps converged on an area northeast of the Task Force.

The clincher was when our aircraft returned from its *Shush Mission*. Although our pilot was sworn to secrecy, even from us, he couldn't help dropping heavy hints that they'd found something very important. His operator was bursting at the seams to get the info to Task Force and spoke in guarded syllables over the phone before leaping aboard his landrover and speeding away in a cloud of dust. That was a dead giveaway. A little imagination and a few more pencil strokes on our map completed the picture. The VC were working up for an all-out attack on Nui Dat.

What really confirmed this in our minds, however, was our own enemy activity barometer, one Private "Shagger" Tomkins. This fellow had a sixth sense that warned him when trouble was brewing. Shagger was a thin rakish lad who looked nervous in his sleep. We'd suspect something was amiss whenever he came to the CP to ask permission to fire his weapon in our test pit. Test firing was a regular procedure; however, before a weapon was fired the Task Force CP had to be advised. It was a simple precaution that avoided nearby units thinking an attack was under way and all hell breaking loose.

Shagger's intuition must have worked like a radio receiver; picking up bad vibes from the telephones and radios around the Task Force before sounding the alarm when enough data had been absorbed. This particular afternoon, when Shagger lobbed grim-faced into our CP, we knew the true reason he needed to test his weapon was to boost his confidence. Sergeant Brown gave him the nod then advised Task Force. A few minutes later the sharp *crack-crack-crack* of Shagger's SLR echoed through the rubber trees.

Test firing a weapon always presents a quandary for the user. Once fired, Army discipline says the weapon must be cleaned: once cleaned, the user wants to make sure the weapon works — so he's tempted to test fire it again. This could easily lead to an endless loop of fire, clean, fire . . .

As I said, we knew that whenever Shagger was getting the vapours he'd test his weapon. The SLR's solid feel, the response to the pressure on the trigger and the sight of the rounds gouging holes in the ground turned Shagger into a super soldier — temporarily. He'd go away, clean his weapon, then his subconscious would again hear the tom-toms beating. Shortly after he'd be back for another test. Shagger Tomkins wasn't a coward, he just spooked a little easier than others. Test firing was his way of overcoming fear. I think we were grateful to Shagger because he acted as a catalyst that relieved our own tension: by reassuring him everything was going to be okay we were actually boosting our own self-confidence.

So although his appearance provoked a few jibes, the word spread, inspiring a rash of weapon testing throughout the unit as others decided to blow the cobwebs from their barrels — just in case. By 1600hrs a minor battle was in progress at our test pit.

I tossed up whether I should blast off a few rounds myself, but my attention was diverted by a phone call from Task Force. It was Queeg, demanding to know whether the afternoon's courier aircraft from Saigon was carrying the mail. I used the phone to check with our control tower. The controller advised that the Caribou was about to land and its pilot had confirmed they had the mail on board. I passed this on to Queeg and was surprised that he seemed genuinely grateful. I guess he too was sweating on news from home. Maybe he was human after all. The prospect of mail cheered me. I temporarily forgot about the imminent danger — real or imagined.

Seventy-Six Trombones . . .

Mike Dawson

I wondered if there would be a brass band to welcome us on arrival at Nui Dat. After all, *I* was about to contribute my considerable skills to the war effort and once the Vietcong heard the news they'd realise theirs was a hopeless cause. At least, that's what my ego was telling me.

Instead, the Caribou dropped steeply in a combat approach, slammed onto the runway, slowed under reverse thrust then turned off onto a dusty area at the side of the strip. As the aircraft screeched to a halt the loadmaster hit the ramp switch and the door whined open. "C'mon, everybody out!" he yelled impatiently. "We have to get the hell out of here before the attack!"

"Attack! What attack?" I called to him above the spluttering engines.

"The fucking place is on full alert. They expect an attack at any time," he bawled as we shuffled towards the exit.

Jesus, we're walking right into it, I thought as sunlight and dust swirled around us. Clutching our duffles and blinking against the glare we stumbled out into the dust storm kicked up by the idling propellers. There was a cluster of open-cab landrovers nearby. As we jumped from the hold they backed impatiently up to the aircraft, nudging us aside. The drivers began loading the mail. We were ignored; all attention seemed focused on those damn sacks as they were piled high on each vehicle.

I battled through the crowd until I was clear of the dust storm. I looked around, wide-eyed, searching for a familiar face. I saw a sergeant rounding up men for one of the battalions, but no one from my unit.

"Where's One-Six-One, Sergeant?" I yelled at the sweating, dust-streaked NCO.

He looked at my new jungle uniform, flashed me the look a policeman gives a lost child and pointed to the northern side of the runway. "That's them."

Through the dust haze I could see a row of tin sheds among tall rubber trees. There were light aircraft on the flight line nearby. The burned out husk of a Sioux helicopter sat on the edge of the runway. I couldn't help staring at it. It was the remains of one of the aircraft I was here to fly.

"No one has three hundred and sixty-five days to go," the sergeant called with a shake of his head. I bristled at the remark, but knew it was part of the initiation. I smiled weakly, realising I'd soon be confronted with a barrage of similar jibes. The sergeant winked and strode off towards a landrover.

The Caribou finished unloading, then blew another dust storm as it impatiently taxied back onto the runway. The engines throttled up and the green transport clattered down the strip, lifted its nose and galloped into the sky.

They seem in an awful hurry to clear out, I thought as I watched it climb steeply away. Suddenly I realised it was my last tangible link with home and felt unexpectedly apprehensive. This was the place that so often headed the six o'clock news, and it was going to be under attack at any moment! I was being thrown in at the deep end. What a hell of an introduction.

I hitched my duffle over my shoulder and hurried towards 161 Flight. As I crossed the runway I was aware of sounds previously cloaked by the Caribou's engines. The distinctive snap of small arms fire echoed from 161's lines. Behind me an artillery battery cracked rounds overhead.

Jesus Christ! I thought as I looked for a place to take cover. *It's happening now, the VC are coming through the wire and I'm unarmed!*

Ned Kelly

As the Caribou droned into the afternoon sky, I remembered that not only had it flown in the mail, but it should have brought John Devlin's replacement. I walked to the CP entrance to see if I could spot the newcomer — I wanted to be the first to give Mike Dawson the standard three-sixty-five-days-to-go sucker greeting.

A mud-plastered apparition carrying a duffle bag squelched across the flight line. Beneath the grime I recognised Mike Dawson. "What happened to him?" I muttered.

One of the ground crew standing nearby obliged. "He was crossing the airstrip when he suddenly ran and jumped in the drainage ditch."

Odd behaviour, I thought. Then I saw Shagger Tomkins striding confidently back from the weapon test pit. I realised what had happened. Mike was suffering from over-training brought on by a three week stint at the Army's Jungle Warfare Centre prior to departure. There, reflexes were sharpened so that at the first sound of gunfire the reaction was instinctive. Mike wasn't the first to have sought refuge in the ditch. Too bad it was full of mud.

Tomkins spotted Mike and, without realising he was the cause of the new officer's dishevelment, straightened up and snapped a crisp salute. Mike fumbled with his duffle and managed to wave a grimy right arm as if shooing flies.

"No one has three hundred and sixty-five days to go, sir," Shagger brazenly added. I suppressed a grin as I watched him straighten up, suddenly supremely confident — he realised that here was an officer who was probably more terrified of the place than he was. Shagger marched off towards his tent, leaving me wondering if his intuition was right.

Sure enough, a few minutes later Task Force HQ was on the horn. All unit representatives were to report to the HQ briefing room by 1615hrs. Word had come through that a NVA regiment was moving to attack nui Dat.

My immediate response was, "What, *again*?" We'd become a little blase about Task Force's frequent prophecies of doom. But we also knew that it was better to be over-cautious than to be overrun. With two battalions away and most units having sent a major slice of their manpower to support operations in Ben Hoa, we were vulnerable. I thought it particularly ironic that because we'd successfully cleaned up Phuoc Tuy Province, we could spare troops to help the Americans in their area. Now *we* were drawing the crabs! In war it just doesn't pay to be efficient.

As Operations Officer it was my place to attend the briefing. I waited until the mail was delivered to the orderly room then hovered impatiently as the clerks sorted the envelopes. There were two for me — one smelling of perfume, which I knew as a harbinger of welcome news. I stuffed the letters in my pocket. They'd have to wait until after the briefing. I buckled on my pistol belt and headed for our landrover.

VUNG TAU

On arrival at Vung Tau, Sergeant Bucknell was whisked from the chopper into the Australian First Field Hospital. By this time Bucknell firmly believed the only way the bullet he'd swallowed was going to come out was via a surgical incision. In fact a surgical team was waiting, scalpels poised. As soon as they began prepping him, however, the error was discovered.

"I've got a damned good mind to go in after it anyway," the

surgeon threatened, clicking the jaws of a shiny steel rib spreader. "That will teach those whackers up at Nui Dat to get their casualty classifications right!"

Bucknell was a brave soldier who'd seen plenty of action in his career, but the sight and smell of these antiseptic surroundings, the neat rows of sharp needles and other Torquemada devices evoked a primitive terror far greater than any muddy, bloody battle could ever have done. He wasn't used to people who actually dismantled human beings with clinical precision; he was more at home with dismemberment by force. He leapt, Lazarus-like, from the stretcher and bolted for the door.

The surgical team saw the humour of the situation. They caught up with Bucknell in the corridor and assured the white-faced NCO they weren't going to vivisect him. Instead, the doctor prescribed a schooner of industrial-strength laxative and made Bucknell drain the glass. He was then issued with a bed-pan, told to wait in the toilet block and not to come back until he'd produced the bullet.

By late afternoon, Bucknell was a desiccated husk. But at last he was rewarded with the metallic clink of the cartridge being expelled. He showered, then triumphantly showed the shining bullet to the Medical Officer. The MO signed off his paperwork and told Bucknell he could return to his unit.

Bucknell found that getting back to Nui Dat by nightfall wasn't possible. The roads were closed and the only way was by air. Nui Dat was on full alert and nothing was going in until the following morning. He explained it to the hospital's orderly room and they allocated him a bed overnight.

Bucknell couldn't believe his luck. His misadventure had led to good fortune; he was stranded overnight in Sin City. The only thing was, with hundreds of ripe bar girls to choose from, he had only about ten dollars in Military Script with him. That was enough for a "short time" at one of the flea-bag steam and cream parlours, but, not having been with a lady for almost a month, Bucknell wanted a more meaningful relationship.

He'd heard of a new, up-market establishment known as Madame Vinh's Pleasure Palace and Grill. There, it was said, one received a steak cooked to perfection and a blow-job that threatened to collapse the thickest skull. The price for these delights was thirty bucks. To that he'd need to add the cost of a few drinks — all bar girls needed a little wooing, and the price of Saigon Tea was getting out of hand due to the influx of American soldiers.

He knew he needed to increase his bankroll significantly. There was only one way to do that, particularly with hundreds of Yanks nearby at the 23rd Evac Hospital. As the sun dipped to the horizon, Bucknell spruced himself up, collected a leave pass from the orderly room, then hitched a ride with one of the medical vehicles over to the American hospital. He knew he was bound to find a poker game there.

The Four O'Clock Follies

". . . an NVA force, possibly a regiment, is believed to have moved into Phuoc Tuy province. It is supported by regional VC units, including D445 Battalion which has recently been reinforced . . ."

Extract from Task Force Briefing circa *February 1968*

NUI DAT

Ned Kelly

The Task Force G2 Intelligence read his assessment, then stood back as if waiting for a round of applause. It seemed the more they frightened you, the more efficient our Intelligence people were regarded. According to this officer, the prognosis was very bad. 1 ATF Nui Dat was about to be terminated. His efficiency reports must have been exceptional.

D445 battalion had been whipped in the Battle of Long Tan in '66. Since then they'd roamed the jungle like Oriental Flying Dutchmen, waiting for their chance of revenge. Now they had it. The Task Force perimeter was lightly manned: one battaliion of infantry plus supporting arms. A concentrated thrust at one point could possibly see them break through . . .

These thoughts rattled around my mind as the G2 Int resumed his seat. Normally the afternoon briefing was a dry litany of statistics summarising the day's activity around the Province and throughout Vietnam. Between periods of heavy action, the briefing was almost a social event, with unit commanders competing to score points with the Task Force Commander. The Task Force Commander in turn would use it to demonstrate his wisdom, clear thinking and mastery of all things military — often by crucifying someone he'd found wanting. I lived in terror of being singled out in one of these sessions and held up to ridicule.

Today's briefing, however, had been devoted entirely to the enemy threat materialising on our doorstep. We'd been through similar alerts many times before; mostly they turned out to be false alarms. This time the G2 Int had delivered his missive with convincing sincerity. Seeing that everyone else in Vietnam had been hit hard during the TET offensive, maybe our time *was* up.

The situation was reminiscent of the old American West where the Apaches attack the fort and the settlers hold out until the last bullet. But instead of fortifying our perimeter with old furniture and water barrels, then lying in wait gripping our carbines and reminiscing about Mom back home in her rocking chair, our plan was different.

There was a buzz of conversation as the Task Force Operations Officer stood to deliver his orders. The G2 (OPS) was a tall, slim Major with an Errol Flynn moustache, renowned for his flamboyant performances. He took the lecturn, studiously laid out his papers, then unfolded a collapsible pointer in the manner of duellist unsheathing his rapier. For the benefit of two US pressmen in the audience he explained that the Australian way of foiling an attack was to find the enemy first. With a swish of his pointer, he attacked the map. *En Garde!*

"Our philosophy of patrolling and ambushing likely routes of advance have been proved time and again," he announced as he wielded his weapon. (*Slash-slash*) "Additional fighting patrols are moving out to supplement our regular patrol program. *(Slash-jab)* These are mostly platoon-sized, with reinforcements and artillery on call if contact is made." *(Jab-jab-jab)* The G2 paused with his pointer over his shoulder. "We will supplement the ground patrol program with additional aerial recon." He sought me out — I'd purposely sat as far back in the room as I could to avoid drawing attention, for I feared someone might ask me about Roger's episode with the flags. He aimed his quivering rapier at me. "Lieutenant Kelly, can 161 Flight sustain the reconnaissance program tonight with one aircraft down?"

"We sure can," I parried confidently. *Make 'em think I know what I'm talking about.*

"161 has lost an aircraft?" the Task Force commander interrupted. The Brigadier looked along the row of seats to the far end where Queeg sat brooding.

Uh-oh, I thought. The King hasn't been told yet.

"Yes, sir," Queeg replied sombrely. "Happened about two hours ago. One of their choppers crashed on route 328 after being hit by enemy fire." He glared malevolently in my direction.

"Is the pilot all right?" the Great Panjandrum shifted his steely gaze to me and raised a bushy eyebrow.

"Yes sir, he was picked up by an American Dust-Off," I replied, desperately trying to think how I could change the subject to the weather.

"No injuries?"

"The observer was wounded by shrapnel, but the pilot's fine." That was more than I could say for Roger's barbequed Sioux.

"What brought him down?" the Brigadier asked.

Twenty senior heads were going back and forth like spectators at a tennis match during this question and answer routine. I was getting in deeper with every volley and had become the focus of attention. Queeg stared at me, eyebrows raised. "Yes Lieutenant, what *did* happen?" he added in a sinister tone.

In the front row, still dressed in his grey USAF flight suit, was Jade Zero Six. The Colonel looked at me blank-faced. My preliminary report to Task Force, conveniently leaving out incriminating details, was now on record. Now I was being asked directly. My story had to mesh or Roger, Jade Zero Six and I would be candidates for blindfolds and cigarettes.

I remembered an old soldier's advice to me: *When bullshitting to the brass always make it a whopper.* "We're not sure," I replied with great sincerity. "It might've been an RPG-7 —"

There were suckings of breath around the room. The RPG-7

was a Soviet anti-tank missile, it could punch a hole through a foot of armour plate. But it *had* occasionally been used against helicopters, with spectacular results, all bad.

Jade Zero Six smiled thinly. The Brigadier nodded. "The crew's lucky to be alive. Anyhow, we know you'll do your best tonight."

I breathed easier. Queeg's face bulged red and his eyes narrowed to angry slits. Somehow he knew there was more to this than I'd revealed, but he couldn't put his finger on it. Hopefully by the time the truth leaked out, the incident would be so far in the past that it would be just another war story. In the meantime, maybe Queeg would step on a land mine or something equally debilitating.

The G2 swished his pointer to command attention. "Very well. We all know what has to be done." He turned to the map. "If Charley attacks tonight, chaps, we'll knock him for six!" *(Swish-whack!)*

I restrained a smile. His quote was straight out of Field Marshal Montgomery's memoirs. It was trite, corny, but said with such aplomb that one couldn't help feeling sorry for the enemy.

The G2 balanced his sword-pointer on the toe of his boot. He struck a pose reminiscent of D'Artagnan challenging the Dauphin's lackeys. "Any questions?"

A few hands shot up. The G2 gave answers. Most of the questions were, I suspect, set-ups to make it clear to the members of the press corps that we Aussies knew how to fight the war, whereas the Americans hadn't yet decided whether they were in combat or a varsity football game.

Then the Task Force commander took the podium and fixed us with a paternal look. "A victory against us would be a political coup for the enemy," the Brigadier began. "As this is an election year for the US Presidency, it could seriously affect the United States' commitment to the war —"

"Affect the *US* commitment?" I repeated under my breath. Last thing I was concerned about was LBJ's political skin. (Ironically, a month later LBJ announced he wouldn't be seeking re-election).

"— so if the enemy does attack, they'll be prepared to accept a casualty rate disproportionate to the tactical significance of this base. This point must be driven home to all personnel . . ."

I shuddered. This was a polite way of saying we'd be outnumbered and that every man must be prepared to fight to the death. It was the Alamo Scenario. *Bugler, sound Deguello. Take no prisoners!*

"I will personally inspect units," prior to last light, the Brigadier continued.

I definitely wasn't prepared to make the ultimate sacrifice. I figured my best chance for survival was to be absent from Nui Dat while the slaughter took place. That could be arranged — I'd deal myself into tonight's recon schedule as observer. I was so absorbed with planning my escape I missed the conclusion of the Brigadier's rallying speech. But then, I'd heard it all before.

As we filed from the briefing room I saw Jade Zero Six lurking near the door. The Colonel flashed me a conspiratorial wink, then tipped his baseball cap in salute. I touched my bush hat in response. We didn't speak.

That's how I'll always remember him. A wiry little guy with a lopsided grin who knew how to bend the rules. A few weeks later, Jade Zero Six was directing an airstrike near the coast when his Bird Dog's wing was clipped by an F-4. One of our helicopters saw the accident and followed the spinning aircraft down. Jade Zero Six crashed on the beach. Our pilot was at the wreckage less than a minute later. There was nothing anyone could have done.

VUNG TAU, 1700HRS

Sergeant Bucknell had found what he was looking for. In the recuperation wing of the US 23rd Evac he'd come across a group of eight marines. They had all been caught in a VC ambush and were now in the final stages of recovering from a variety of bullet and shrapnel wounds. One, a huge black man with a Schwarzenegger physique, hands swathed in bandages, lay on his back with a drip feeding into his left arm. Three of the men were sufficiently mobile to be allowed out of bed. Dressed in fatigues, they sat around a table at the far end of the ward. They were playing poker.

Bucknell peered through the door's little square window. The table was stacked with chips and littered with cash. It was a rich game. But how could he buy in with only ten bucks? He looked at the soldiers. One was a pug-nosed sergeant about Bucknell's vintage — the others were young PFCs. It looked as if it was the sergeant's game: most of the loot was piled in front of him.

Bucknell figured he knew how to handle the situation. He waited until the hand finished. Then, as the dealer was collecting the cards, he pushed the door open. "Have any of you blokes seen Sergeant Murphy?" he asked in the broadest Australian accent he could muster.

"Moiphy?" snorted the pug-nosed Sergeant as he scooped his winnings. He looked suspiciously at Bucknell. "Don't know any Moiphy around here — what's his outfit?"

"82nd Airborne. They told me he was in this ward. I've got five hundred dollars for him." Bucknell grinned sheepishly at the American sergeant. The marine had a name tag pinned to his chest. It was J.J. Ferraro.

J.J. Ferraro smiled. "You an Aussie?" He pronounced the word as "Ossy". His voice was deep and rasping. When he sucked breath, his flattened nose whistled like a tea kettle.

"Yeah, just down from The Dat so they can check an old wound." Bucknell clutched his stomach. He could see his mark was sniffing the lure. "I promised Murphy I'd bring him his money. He won it fair and square in a poker game down here two weeks ago. He said to call it quits but I want him to have it."

"Hell yeah, I wouldn't turn down five hundred bucks. Where is this Moiphy guy, anyhow — maybe he can give me a loan." Ferraro chuckled. He took the bait. "Say, meanwhile until he shows, why don't you join us?"

Bucknell looked contemplative. Ferraro reminded him of a Mafia hood, he'd look at home wearing a black shirt, white tie and Fedora. Bucknell shook his head. "I can't. I've left my money over at the Australian Hospital."

"Hey Aussie, your credit's good here. We're all allies in this fucked out war." Ferraro pushed a pile of red chips across the table. "Here's a hundred to start with."

They all shook hands and made quick introductions. Bucknell

eased himself into a chair opposite Ferraro. The three Americans smiled broadly, thinking they'd just hooked a sucker from down under. Little did they know they were reeling in a White Pointer.

Yea though I walk through the valley of the shadow of death, I fear no evil, for I am the biggest bad-ass in the valley
>   Scrawled beneath the sign at the entrance to the USAF Third Air Division, Anderson AFB, Guam.

ANDERSON AFB, GUAM, 1700HRS

Six B-52 bombers hauled themselves from the runway and smoked into the evening sky. Each of the giant aircraft carried sixty four-hundred-kilo bombs stowed in their bomb bays and slung beneath their swept wings. After topping fuel tanks from waiting KC-135 tankers, the B-52s continued climbing until they'd reached forty thousand feet. The sortie would last almost twelve hours. Their target: a North Vietnamese regiment, somewhere in South Vietnam.

The mission was known as an *"Arc-Light"* strike. After the long haul to Vietnam the B-52s would be guided over their target by radar based at the Ben Hoa Airfield. The accuracy of these strikes was estimated at less than a hundred metres, enabling their bombs to be concentrated over a small area.

Of all the weapons used against the VC and NVA, these B-52 strikes were the most feared. Flying at high altitude, the big aircraft couldn't be seen or heard on the ground. Their bombs, released from an altitude of almost eight miles, were travelling faster than sound when they hit. There was no piercing shriek to warn of their approach, just a wave of explosions that blasted through the jungle leaving a pockmarked swathe of smouldering red earth.

When flying over South Vietnam, the B-52s were untroubled by enemy fighters or SAMs. So these missions were a milk run, allowing the crew to concentrate on flying the aircraft and achieving maximum bombing accuracy. With meteorological conditions being updated continuously and release sequences computer controlled, their bombs would spread evenly across the target area. Hardly a square metre of ground would remain untouched.

NVA and VC regiments had frequently been caught in these rolling bomb carpets. Days after a raid, jibbering black-eyed survivors, bleeding from their ears, nose and anus, had often been found wandering the jungle. Some were too far gone to recover and were mercifully despatched with a bullet through their scrambled brain. Those who could still talk told of the stark terror of being caught in the bomb storm.

Arc Light strikes depended on accurate intelligence to pinpoint their target areas. Often, due to VC counter intelligence, the information was false, resulting in acres of jungle being pulped. Tonight, however, as the six bombers settled into the long flight ahead, their crews were confident this would be a good mission. The information for the strike was classified A1. It had come from the Australians operating in Phuoc Tuy Province. They had a reputation for understating the situation and the briefing for tonight's mission indicated they had an entire NVA regiment on toast.

Accordingly a strike originally planned to support the Marine base at Khe Shan was quickly rescheduled for the Australians' target. Leading the formation was a veteran bomber pilot who'd seen action over Germany and Japan in the Second World War. Painted on the nose of his aircraft, was the inscription: *Old Bad Ass*.

NUI DAT, 1700HRS

Ned Kelly

The mood at 161 Flight changed to sceptical anticipation when I returned with the news we were doomed. The second in command called all officers and senior NCOs together for a planning conference. Within twenty minutes everyone knew what they had to do. We'd been through so many similar operations most of us could recite the procedure in our sleep.

Our main task would be to keep two aircraft on patrol during the night. While this might seem relatively simple, it required a mountain of detail to be covered. We'd use a combination of fixed- and rotary-wing, with the fixed-wing carrying our solitary night vision aid, the Starscope I'd acquired from the Americans by trading slouch hats and beer.

The maintenance crew had repaired John Devlin's aircraft, fitting new rotor blades and replacing other damaged components in under three hours. The aircraft had been test flown and was now on the flight line. That gave us two helicopters and two fixed-wing for tonight's effort. We'd fly them two-about — one Sioux and one Cessna airborne at a time.

There were also the ground crews to be seen to. They'd have to tend the aircraft without showing lights that could draw sniper fire. Not the least consideration was setting the runway flarepath; Luscombe Field didn't have electric lighting. The "Lights-runway, portable, battery operated" our QM had requisitioned were never supplied. "Pots-flare, kerosene. Outdoor entertainment, insect repelling" were sent instead, along with a worrying memo from some Canberra thick-head stating that electric runway lights were only for issue to "permanent establishments" and reminding us that Nui Dat should not be considered as such.

"Look at it this way, zur," the QM had rationalised. "At least the h'airfield will be free of mosquitoes."

Shorrock had a point, but it meant that rather than flick a switch, the flarepath had to be lit and extinguished by hand. On an airstrip watched by enemy, it was time consuming and dangerous. Our fire crew had the dubious honor of tending the flarepath in their fire "engine" — a make-do collection of extinguishers cobbled onto a landrover chassis, another legacy of our creaking procurement system. And because of the time taken to tend the lights, the strip, once lit, became a perfect aiming point for enemy rocket or mortar fire.

In addition to operating our aircraft, we had to man our area's defences. After the initial one hundred per cent stand-to, lasting from a half-hour before last night until an hour after, we'd maintain a fifty per cent alert. Half our available manpower would be in their defensive positions while the other rested. They'd swap over every three hours. Despite the blackout, the evening movie would be screened in the soldier's mess; those waiting to go on duty might as well be watching a movie as staring into space in their tents. Tonight's movie, fittingly, was *War and Peace* — the complete, uncut Soviet version, almost five hours of celluloid drama.

We knew this would be one of those cow's guts nights — dark and clammy. Even the most hardened soldier becomes jittery at night. Waiting for the Yellow Peril to come screaming through the wire while barely able to see their hands in front of their faces, a big problem would be avoiding an accidental shooting. That's where the experience of our senior NCOs was invaluable. Many of them had seen action in Korea and Malaya and for them this was just another late night at the office.

I checked our task board. I'd be flying two sorties as observer in one of our fixed-wing aircraft. No doubt during the night Queeg would be on the phone every few minutes with his incessant demands, so I looked forward to being out of his firing line for a few hours. And of course if the big massacre did take place, hopefully I'd be a couple of thousand feet up in the sky at the time. At least I'd be doing something useful, I told myself. Maybe I'd be able to detect the approaching bad guys and the base would be saved. Which reminded me — "Batteries," I called to Dave Brown. "The starscope needs fresh batteries." Last night's recons had almost drained them. They were special cells made only for the starscope. Without them the scope was useless — *and* I'd be stuck on the ground at the mercy of the VC.

"Maybe the QM has some," Dave replied.

Damn it! Last thing I wanted was to match wits with Shorrock at this late hour. The starscope was a sore point with him. It was a piece of non-issue equipment that mocked his carefully indexed, cross-filed, back-speaking world. He was quite piqued that I'd gone over his head to scrounge one, regarding my action as an affront to his status of chief procurer.

Reluctantly I picked up the phone, cranked the handle and was switched through to the QM's empire.

"Ahar, Staff Sergeant Shorrock speaking," the QM answered in a booming voice.

"QM, I need fresh batteries for the starscope," I demanded.

"The what-scope, zur?"

"The *starscope*, QM." I knew the one-eyed pirate was toying with me.

"Ahem . . . I don't believe we have a scope-Star on our equipment table, zur."

"I know we don't, QM, but I have one here in the command post and I have to use it tonight. Can you get us some new batteries — please?"

"Well zur, maybe I can get some from the quarty master Sergeant at the American 175 gun battery. They have scopes-star on inventory."

"Good."

"But one favour deserves another, zur."

"Such as?" Here comes the sting, I thought.

"He's been asking if he could be flown out to Xuyen Moc village —"

"What in hell for?" Xuyen Moc seemed very popular today.

"Appears he's got a young lady out there, zur."

"A lady?" So that was it. Xuyen Moc was a love hamlet. No wonder we'd rushed to its relief. So much for defending democracy.

"He wants to check and see if she be all right."

"Okay, okay!" I replied. What did I care if yet another American was porking a local girl. If the Americans fought as hard as they fucked, the war would've been over years ago. "I'll see if one of tomorrow's recons can drop him off."

"Thank you, zur, I'll phone back in a few minutes."

I hung up, wondering if the Yank Quartermaster Sergeant spoke terms of endearment backwards to his Vietnamese popsy. Maybe he did *everything* backwards. It was too bizarre to comprehend.

The phone rang. Dave answered. The batteries for the Starscope would be here within fifteen minutes, Shorrock advised, adding that his American friend would be along in the morning to be flown to the embrace of his woman. There was no doubt about it, I acknowledged. The world's Armies were run by NCOs. We officers only thought we were in charge. I wish I'd been smart enough to organise a morning of passion after tonight's siege. It seemed very civilised.

Carefully I took the starscope from its padded case and checked it. The black tube was a compact piece of electronic wizardry that allowed the user to see in the dark. Word was it cost about five thousand dollars. To me that was almost two years' pay. Yet I'd traded it for a few slouch hats and six cases of beer. I wondered what I could do if I really tried? Maybe a helicopter of my own — I'd heard of such deals in Saigon. In war, it seemed, money was no object, at least for the Americans. Gingerly, I replaced the precious instrument in its case. Thank God it didn't officially belong to us. If it had, the damn thing would've been kept locked away and never used for fear of incurring the wrath of the Canberra bean counters if it was damaged. Or else I'd have been made personally responsible for it. That was the Army way.

I peered out of the door of the CP towards the airfield as two RAAF helicopters lifted off and scurried towards Vung Tau. That was a sure sign trouble was afoot; Nine Squadron had a policy of being as far away from any coming action as they could possibly manage. The irony was that after the RAAF bugged out, a US Army Dust-Off Huey would fly in and remain on standby to provide us with medical evacuation during the night.

I could feel the tension growing. Even though we'd been through these alerts many times, there's something unnerving in the knowledge that someone *out there* wants to kill you. No matter what your training or how macho you felt, there always came a time when the reality of the situation confronted you. This was a war, and it was the enemy's job to kill us, just as it was our job to kill them. It's a sad, oppressive feeling and one that always gripped me at sunset.

Our CP radios began crackling with calls as coms were tested between units. We drew our blackout curtains, checked our torches and weapons. Shagger Tomkins ran himself through one last fire/clean/fire cycle, but this time he had to get in the queue. A minor battle raged at our test pit — and a dozen others around the Task Force. The snare-drum rattle of M-16s and the castanet crack of SLRs blended with the base-drum thump of outgoing artillery registering defensive fire zones. Like an orchestra before a concert, the Task Force was tuning its instruments.

As the sun nudged the horizon an eerie silence fell. Nui Dat was as ready as it would ever be. I gathered my notes, marked the wall map and prepared to brief our pilots.

The target for tonight is . . .
Lieutenant Greg McBride

I'll always remember the briefing before that night's flying began. All pilots, observers and operations staff gathered in our command post, waiting to learn what Task Force HQ was up to. With only seven pilots left it was a modest affair, lightened by typical Aussie humour.

Ned Kelly approached the wall map with a grim look and pointed to it with an old billiard cue. "Tonight's mission —"

"God no, not Berlin again!" someone interrupted.

"No, Carstairs," a fake British voice piped up. "It's the ruddy ball-bearing factory."

"You can't do this to us, the night fighters — the flak — horrible!" another wailed as everyone started humming *Off We Go Into the Wild Blue Yonder*.

Ned could never resist the temptation to play-act. He whacked the map with his billiard cue, then strutted about like a Nazi martinet. "You *dumbkoffs* is all wronk!" he exhorted. "Der objectif iz der *Poopen-Farten* cuckoo clock verks. Dis time you vill be bombink der assembly line vere dey make der liddle birts vot pop ouder der clock unt go, *cuckoo*. Mitout cuckoo birts der enemy's *Blitzkreig* will be *kaput* because dey vill not vake up in time to catch der mornink Kombi-bus to der trenches."

"*Jahwohl, mein Fuhrer*," I shouted.

"*Sieg Heil, Sieg Heil*!" we all joined in.

At that point the Task Force commander strode into the Command Post. We froze. Ned was standing with his back to the entrance and thought our sudden stern looks were in response to his cajoling. It inspired him to even greater heights of creative acting. He flapped his arms about in a comic Hitler parody. "*Achtung, dumbkoffs!* Your *Focker-fliegvagens* iz der best machinens der dopey *Fockers* in Canberra can supply from der *Focking* petty cash tin. Zo —" He paused and turned. "Shit!" he gasped as he faced the Brigadier.

"I beg your pardon," the Brigadier politely demanded.

"I mean, shit *sir*!" Ned sprang to attention, billiard cue at his side like a Brown Bess musket.

"That's better," said the Brigadier, forcing back a smile that threatened to fracture his composure. "It's good to see that morale in this unit is high. We're counting on you tonight. Carry on." He turned and left without another word.

Ned didn't skip a beat. He shrugged then rattled off more ersatz German. "You vill *not* ask me any questions!" he concluded in a sinister voice. "Because I gotta change my jockey shorts before I go flying."

We all cracked up as Ned threw a *Sieg Heil*, then waddled from the CP.

I can't over-emphasise the importance of humour to us all. In a country where the chief comedian was a General by the name of Westmoreland, we needed every laugh we could get. It acted as a safety valve for pent up tension, and that evening we were all feeling bloody jumpy at the prospect of becoming political sacrifices.

Tomfoolery dispersed with, the briefing got down to serious business. Ned returned to the map, this time all pretence at humour gone. There was a sudden, expectant air, and tension started building again. We were privy to information that most other units had been denied: Task Force HQ suspected they'd located a NVA base to the north-east. Tonight there'd be a B-52 strike on the area.

Now all the pieces came together. The target was in a stretch of thick jungle we'd been keeping a cautious eye on for almost four months. It was encouraging to see that at last someone at Task Force HQ was taking notice of us.

The strike was due at around 2200hrs. Meanwhile we'd patrol out to line Bravo, then pay special attention to likely routes of approach from our north and north-east. We were not to overfly the target area until after the strike. A large buffer zone had been drawn around the target. I sketched it on my map. We were to stay outside the safety zone, not only because it might spook the enemy, but also for our own safety. None of us wanted to be caught in a shower of bombs dropped from forty thousand feet — even if they were "friendly".

I'd drawn two sorties of more than three hours each — total flying time longer than a WW2 Berlin run. In some ways I think I'd have preferred to fly a Lancaster to Berlin and back, because flying a single-engined aircraft over the jungle at night is unnerving business. The possibility of an engine failure was always present. It was bad enough during the day, but at night, unless the engine quit near a road or a paddy field, the prospect of surviving a forced landing into the jungle was slim. And we didn't carry parachutes — the issue was still being debated by the Canberra policy makers.

It was a revival of the World War One argument which stated "a pilot's job is to stick with his aeroplane". Apart from the fact that the question had been resolved almost fifty years ago in favour of parachutes, I would have thought it was a simple matter of personal choice. Of course, for helicopter crews parachutes were impractical — the chances of being sliced through the rotor blades like a celery stick were greater than the risks involved with riding the chopper down. But for fixed-wing crews, particularly at night, parachutes were a practical means of survival. Word had it the chiefs lived in terror of a nervous young pilot prematurely bailing out and leaving a plane load of brass hats drifting around the sky. Apparently it never occurred to them that maybe the passengers should carry parachutes too.

Our aircraft also lacked equipment for night reconnaissance. The Cessna itself was an extremely reliable and tough little bird, but its avionics were very basic. The only night vision aid we had — a starscope — was a help, but not much. Requests for night vision equipment and more effective radios had been met with the usual rebuffs from the system and we'd given up trying.

Compounding this was the danger of ground fire. Our aircraft were constantly being fired on during the day, but the technique of low flying minimised exposure time and accuracy. But at night, flying at a higher altitude, aircraft were a better target. Fortunately, except for moonlit nights, our aircraft were difficult to see — painted dark green and with navigation lights off, they merged with the darkness. Tonight there would be no moon, so ground fire shouldn't be a problem. But lurking in the back of all our minds were Intelligence reports that the VC were being equipped with Soviet radar-controlled anti-aircraft guns and shoulder-launched heat seeking missiles. It was only a matter of time before they reached our area.

After the briefing I went to the flight line to check my aircraft, preferring to do it while there was still daylight rather than stumble around in the dark. I knew the ground crew had done their best and the aircraft would be as near perfect as it was possible to be under such conditions, but I wanted to be sure — night flying wasn't the time for something to come adrift.

I finished my pre-flight inspection then went and sat on a row of sandbags bordering the flight line. As the sun dropped to the horizon, the air cooled. I could feel the heat seeping from the sandbags and steel planking covering the ground. A silence had gripped the base. There was hardly a sound, just the chatter of insects and the occasional crisp echo of a distant radio. Even the ground crew spoke in selfconscious whispers that became softer as the light faded. It was as if they were afraid of drawing the enemy's attention.

There was always a feeling of cautious excitement before a night sortie. It was somehow reminiscent of World War Two. Waiting on the flight line while the sun slid to the horizon evoked strong images of what it must have been like in those days. Even our little Cessnas looked warlike, their propellors silhouetted against the sunset, rocket tubes loaded and ready.

I knew this was the end of an era: ours were the last of a line of piston-engined reconnaissance aircraft whose ancestry could be traced back to World War One. Very little had changed during the intervening years. Sure, we had radios and our aircraft were made of metal rather than wood and fabric, but we did the job the same way — relying on our eyes to find the enemy. But all this was changing. Computers and electronics would replace us in the next war. Robot would hunt robot. At twenty-three I was already obsolete.

At about 1815hrs my observer walked down from the CP. Ned Kelly stashed his equipment in the aircraft then strolled over and sat beside me. I had to hand it to Ned, he was always eager for action, rarely missing an opportunity to fly with us. He was a big man, over six foot four, lean and muscled. Just having him aboard during night recon was reassuring. If we went into the jungle he'd be handy to have around.

We talked quietly, comparing the news from home that had arrived with the evening mail. After a while we both succumbed to the growing tension and waited in silence.

By 1830hrs the sun was a half-disk on the horizon. The silence was heavy; even the artillery had stopped its harrasment fire as if conserving strength for things to come. I took a final quick look around the aircraft, pulled the pins on the rocket tubes, then climbed aboard. Ned strapped into the right hand seat beside me, dragged on his headset, then gave me a thumbs up.

I signalled the ground crew, primed the engine then hit the starter. Our war was on.

1830HRS

Ned Kelly

We took off into an easterly breeze that came with the sunset. There were no clouds and already a few stars pricked the sky as Greg climbed the Cessna to three thousand feet. The air had cooled and I was grateful for the warmth provided by my flack jacket.

We'd worked out a patrol route that would initially take us over the coast. There was little we could do until dark — we knew the VC wouldn't be stupid enough to expose themselves until they felt confident we couldn't see them. So, knowing they'd probably watched us take off, we'd give the impression that the coast was the area we were interested in. As soon as it was dark, though, we'd head inland.

After a few minutes we sighted the beach. It was already softened by the approaching night: a strip of fading gold merging into an indigo sea. The cockpit reflected the sunset behind us, and for a moment I forgot we were participants in a war. I sat, puzzled by the contrast; night recon often provided some of the most beautiful scenes I've ever experienced.

One of my most vivid memories was of a similar night sortie several months ago: we were at three thousand feet, the engine throttled back to a whisper, hardly making headway against a stiff north wind as we loitered above the mouth of the Song Rai river. We were trying to catch sampans running supplies inland. While we watched, a huge golden moon burst above the horizon. It shimmered into the sky, painting the ocean and coastline with light. The surf sparkled against the beach and behind it the Song Rai wound inland to the horizon like a flat silver snake.

We'd turned the ADF receiver into Armed Forces Radio. They were playing the instrumental theme *Love is Blue*. The music fitted the scene as if it had been written for the moment. In headsets that normally echoed with urgent commands, the melody sounded distant, like a fond memory of childhood. We flew on in wordless silence, totally entranced by the incongruous beauty around us. Then the music faded. AFVN's evening news began with the announcer cheerfully reading the day's body count as if he was reciting football scores. The spell was broken, but that tune will forever remind me of flying at night above the South China Sea. Three minutes of enchantment that have never been equalled.

This moonless night in February, however, all I could hear in my headset was the background whine of electronics and radio calls from distant American aircraft, a constant reminder that we weren't the only ones out hunting tonight.

We reached the coast and turned south as the last pool of sunlight drained from the horizon. The jungle was plunged into darkness. Ahead, just below the nose, I could see the lights of Vung Tau. "Lucky bastards," I said over the intercom. "All the whore-houses are doing a roaring trade while we're stuck up here."

"War is hell," Greg replied as we began a slow turn back up the coast. The air was smooth, with only an occasional heat bubble drifting up to shake the aircraft. Out to sea the flashes of a ship's guns were clearly visible as they pounded the mountains on the northern horizon. Tiny red smudges marked the shells' impact. I wondered who was dying.

I tuned the ADF to Armed Forces Radio, hoping to recapture some magic. But it was between-program time with fill-ins; VD and clean-your-weapon commercials assaulted us. Then came a real treat, a pep-talk by General Westmoreland:

"American soldiers and brave Allies," Westy began. "Let me tell you that your efforts and sacrifices during this treacherous Communist offensive —"

I can't remember much of what he said, but I know I'd heard it all before. After Westy finished ("Goodnight brave Americans . . . and allies, whoever . . . ahem . . . wherever you are"), there was a chorus of Bronx cheers on the emergency frequency as American pilots all over Vietnam voiced their appreciation.

"Get yourself a blow job, General!" the shuddering voice of a chopper pilot shouted.

"Hey man, just get us out of this fuckin' place!" another pleaded.

The hubbub continued for a few minutes then subsided. The guard frequency returned to a soft hiss in the background. It was an eye-opener as to how many pilots tuned to AFVN during combat sorties.

Armed Forces Radio, unaware of its audience's response, was determined to spoil our evening by continuing in its propaganda mode. Instead of music, the announcer introduced the senior US Army Chaplain. The chief skypilot was touring the war zone and wanted to add his own words of enlightenment.

There followed a longwinded, fiery blast by Super Padre who talked at high speed without pausing for a breath while reassuring us what a great job we were doing which will teach the North Vietnamese heathens not to fuck with Uncle Sam because God and Mickey Mouse were with us and with such agents of righteousness at our sides we should go forth and kick ass for the Lord. Hallelujah, amen and goodnight, brave soldiers of Christ.

So with our morale boosted and souls polished, we flew on into the night.

When at night they beat retreat,
Hey lydee lydee-lo
All marines they beat their meat,
Hey girl, I miss you so . . .

VUNG TAU

Sgt Bucknell was winning the poker game. After a cautious start which saw him drop fifty dollars in the first three hands, he'd gauged his opponents' style. They were no amateurs, but then neither was Bucknell. He'd learned poker as a youth in the goldfields of Kalgoorlie, where they played with a deadly purpose that would intimidate a Las Vegas casino dealer.

The Americans, though, took some getting used to. Their style tended to be more flamboyant, they played a wider variety of games and — as he'd found in his first tour of '65 — they tended to bluff more than Australians. However, a full house, a flush or a straight, still had the same value. Once Bucknell learned to interpret his opponents' mannerisms, his luck turned.

After the sixth hand he'd won sufficient to pay back Ferraro's grubstake and still have enough to keep going. He lost a few hands then cracked a big pot in a drawn out showdown that saw the two PFCs fold after helping blow out the table stakes.

"Guys, I think we've been had," Ferraro said coolly as Bucknell scooped the pool.

"Now what makes you think that?" Bucknell couldn't restrain a grin from creasing his lips. He'd won almost four hundred dollars — more than a month's pay.

There was tension in the air. The American looked the Australian up and down. The "Ossy" was a big man, not thickset like many Americans, but tall and raw boned — a kind of downunder Garry Cooper. And as he'd learned in idle table talk, this was the man's second tour. He wasn't to be trifled with. "Just a feeling that tells me you're some kind of shill," Ferraro replied slowly.

Bucknell fixed his opponent with a cold stare. "Listen, mate, I don't know what a 'shill' is, but if you're suggesting I'm cheating . . ." He let the words hang, realising that he had to cash in his winnings. Madame Vinh didn't take plastic poker chips. The folding money was at Ferraro's elbow. Last thing he wanted was to have to fight his way out of the hospital.

"I'm saying you're not the innocent loser you made yourself out to be." Ferraro could feel that all eyes in the ward were on him. This was becoming a matter of face. He was a Marine — America's finest — he couldn't be seen to back down, even to an Australian.

Bucknell smiled. "Never pretended to be, now did I. All I needed was enough for a night on the town."

"Shit man! You're saying you can get out of this fuckin' place?"

"Of course I can. I'm staying at the Australian Evac Hospital — not here." Bucknell pulled his leave pass from his breast pocket and flashed it. "Good for twenty-four hours."

"Jesuus! And you're going to get laid with *our fucking money*?"

"Can you think of a better use?"

"Goddam it, I haven't touched pussy in more'n two months."

"Shit man, none of us have!" A voice from one of the beds groaned. "It's been so long I've fallen in love with my hand."

"Hell yeah," the black PFC with the drip in his arm and bandaged hands added. "The sound of you turkeys beatin' your meat keeps me awake till midnight!"

"You're all in a bad way," Bucknell frowned. "Can't you get into Vung Tau somehow?"

"Only us three are allowed out of here" — Ferraro pointed to the men around the table. "But even then we're restricted to the hospital. The Doc says it's another week before he'll let us into town for a blow job."

"Too bad." Bucknell slowly pushed his chips across the table. "Still, maybe, there *is* a way."

Ferraro frowned at the pile of plastic discs. "No way we can get out without passes. Besides, they can't walk far yet." He pointed with thumb over shoulder at the five men in bed.

"I wasn't thinking of getting them *out*." Bucknell said.

"What do you mean?"

"Cash my chips and I'll tell you."

Ferraro paused. "How do I know this isn't a scam?"

"You don't. So try me."

Ferraro shrugged. "I like a man with an honest face." The ice melted as he counted out three hundred and ninety dollars. He pushed it across the table but kept his hand firmly on the cash. "Now tell me."

"Simple. You blokes can't get out of here. But I can. All I have to do is go into Vung Tau and bring the crumpet here."

"Crumpet . . . you mean pussy?" Ferraro's eyebrows threatened to vanish into his crew cut. "You mean *bring the whores in here?*"

"Why not? This is the recupe ward. All I need to know is the timings of the staff rounds and lights out. I can get the girls into the compound, no sweat. I'll slip them in through . . . there." Bucknell pointed to a window beside an empty bed half-concealed by a privacy curtain. "All you have to do is have someone stand watch at the door or fix the night shift. Then you can all go to it."

"Jeesus, you're crazy," Ferraro muttered. "But what the hell, we've nothing to lose by trying!"

Come in, spinner

2050HRS

Ned Kelly

It was one of the darkest nights I could remember. Even the stars seemed reluctant to appear. Instead of the usual bright canopy above us, only a few specks of light seeped through a high veil of cloud that had blown in from the sea. Beneath us the jungle was an inky smudge pierced by lights from villages scattered around the Province. Ahead, sky and ground merged into an oppressive black cloak that wrapped around us and blotted out the horizon. Greg was flying with constant reference to the instruments, for in these conditions the onset of disorientation was often quick and fatal. The only usable reference point was the glow from the lights of Vung Tau.

I had the starscope aimed out of the door. (When on recon the Cessnas flew with the starboard door off to improve visibility.) We'd turned inland and were heading north following route 328, where Roger Colclough had come to grief that afternoon. Through the tube, the ground was a ghostly black and white, tinged with green. As yet I'd sighted nothing.

We were at two thousand feet over flat country, mainly jungle broken by rice fields. The starscope was only good for about a thousand feet. "Can we fly lower?" I called over the intercom.

Greg nodded and cautiously eased the nose down. As we descended the trees took on shape and definition until I could make out individual tree branches. We levelled at a thousand feet.

The starscope could detect the smallest light source: a handheld torch glowed like a beacon at a thousand metres and a lit cigarette could easily be seen at five hundred. On a moonless night, even the cat-eyed VC needed light to move. Their usual practice was to hang a lamp beneath an oxcart so that it shed a dull glow ahead. This was almost invisible to the naked eye except at close range, but through the starscope it became a huge incandescent pool.

I scanned the road's crumbling surface. It was a trembling white strip winding through the rice fields. I noticed a blackened smudge near a bend — the spot where Roger's aircraft had burned. A feeling of dread gripped me. Not wanting to dwell on what could happen if we made a mistake, I checked the fields on either side of the road. Nothing.

We droned on, following the road as it meandered into thick jungle. "Still nothing," I called to Greg after another ten minutes.

"It's early," he replied. His helmeted face reflected the eerie glow from the instruments, giving him an alien appearance.

We flew up and down the highway for another twenty minutes but it was as bare as a new born babe's backside. The trouble was that when the enemy heard our engine all they had to do was pull to the side of the road and pile a few bushes on their vehicles. Even with the scope I wouldn't be able to distinguish a camouflaged truck or an ox-cart from a clump of trees. To do that we needed infra-red equipment. It was available from the Americans, but we couldn't get it until some empire builder in the Defence Department back in Australia ran trials for a year or two. Why they couldn't give it to us to test was beyond me. A few night recons would soon sort it out — even if it only half-worked it would be infinitely better than nothing.

I glanced at the clock on the panel. We'd been airborne for over two hours. Throttled back for maximum endurance, we could hang around for almost four. Tonight we'd change over about every three and a half hours. Any longer and I found myself going cross-eyed from using the scope. Even now, despite regularly switching from left to right eyes, it felt as if the tube was sucking my brain out through my eyeballs.

I lowered the scope. "I need a break," I called to Greg. He nodded; the strain of flying low in these conditions was tiring too. He lifted the nose and we climbed to three thousand feet. There the world seemed even blacker. Only Vung Tau's lights broke the gloom. The additional altitude improved radio reception immensely; we could hear ground stations and aircraft from as far North as the DMZ. As we listened we pieced together the action: someone was being attacked — it sounded like a Marine fire support base — maybe even Khe Sahn. It must have been heavy action as there were two "Spook" AC-47 gunships hosing the perimeter. The ground station was calling for one gunship to direct his fire closer:

"Spook one-six, we need it fifty metres farther west."

"We put it any closer an' you'll be eating our lead yo'self," the AC-47 pilot replied in a Southern drawl.

"Hell man, we're eatin' lead now, them gooks are all over the place like Manhattan hookers on pay night."

"Okay, you got it."

In the background we could hear the gutteral burp of the C-47's mini-guns. This was rivetting stuff, somehow reminiscent of the fifties when, as a kid, I used to lie in front of the radio and listen wide-mouthed to the adventures of Biggles. Only this was *real*, I reminded myself. *Radio theatre, live from the DMZ.*

"Hell, one-six where the fuck did you go?"

"Stand by, we've a problem —"

"You've a fuckin problem! Goddamn, you should see it from down here!"

"We're taking ground fire. Son-of-a-bitch, it's forty mike-mike at least —"

"One-six, we need rounds on the ground now!"

"You mothers are gonna have to wait — goddamn, this is heavy stuff!"

"Hey man, what's goin' down up there? We just saw a big flash in the sky."

"That was us, you dipshit! We're on fire . . . Mayday, Mayday, Mayday . . ."

We could hear the whine of overspeeding propellers.

". . . shee-it! The whole fuckin aircraft's on fire . . ."

The hair on my neck prickled. This beat Biggles any day.

". . . we're goin' in. Oh, Jesus-H-Christ, we're burning, we're burning . . ."

Then from somewhere close, boomed another American voice: "Shut up, one-six and die like a man!"

Greg and I looked at each other. "Better get back to it," he said. I nodded. It was too noisy up here. He dropped the nose and as we descended the voices in our ears faded. We flew north along the road again.

"We'll try closer to the restricted area," Greg suggested. "The B-52 strike's not due for another hour."

After ten minutes we were over the ruins of the village of Thua Tich. In the scope I could see crumbling stone walls and the overgrown foundations of larger buildings, including a temple. Suddenly the scope flared — I'd focused on a bright light. "I've got something!" I called as I tried to locate the source. The picture washed out then seeped back.

Greg banked gently to keep me in position. The tube flared again. I waited for the image to return. When it did, I saw dozens of pinpoints of light streaking across the screen.

Must be a candlelight procession, I thought as I tried to identify the scene. I could hear Greg's voice in the background. I think he was talking to me, but he hadn't pushed his intercom button. I couldn't hear him above the howling engine. *Howling engine?*

I lowered the scope. The aircraft was standing on its port wingtip — I'd been looking straight up at the stars. I looked down. Beneath us green tracer drifted lazily up, then whipped past the aircraft. It was the tracer that had flared the scope. I must've been looking down the barrel of the gun.

"Some bastard's shooting at us!" I yelled over the intercom.

"I wondered when you'd notice!" Greg shouted. His right hand was shoving the throttle through the firewall, while his left dragged the yoke into his stomach. The Cessna pivoted on its wingtip then levelled. The tracers stopped. Greg eased the throttle and circled while he radioed Task Force HQ.

"Possum One Four, maintain surveillance," echoed the taciturn reply.

"What kind of fucking answer is that?" Greg swore as he hauled the aircraft around towards the ruins. He looked at me. "What's the availability of artillery?"

I shook my head. The only artillery that could reach us was the American 175mm mobile guns supporting the Task Force — but they'd been pulled out earlier in the day for the operation around Ben Hoa.

Greg looked at me in exasperation. This was always our problem. We could do little more than wave at the VC.

The radio crackled again. This time I recognised Queeg's voice. "Possum One Four, identify enemy force."

Greg frowned. "He must be kidding."

I shrugged then said, "Maybe if we hang around long enough they'll run up their unit flag."

"One Four, acknowledge!" Queeg demanded.

"Roger," Greg replied as he nudged the aircraft closer to the ruins. We'd climbed to almost two thousand feet. Another stream of tracer chased us. At first the glowing balls of light looked deceptively harmless as they swirled and bobbed like mating fireflies. Then, as if drawn by a magnet, they stretched out into a line and crackled past fifty metres off the starboard wing.

"This is crazy!" Greg muttered as we banked away. The firing stopped. I swept the area with the scope. There was no sign of movement, but then two men and a machine gun didn't take much hiding.

"One Four, report," Queeg demanded.

Greg thumbed the transmit button. "The gun is still firing at us," he answered.

"Can you identify?"

"Definitely unfriendly," Greg replied.

"I need to know whether they are Bravo or Golf persons!" Queeg insisted.

"Bravo or Golf persons?" Greg repeated to me over the intercom. "What's he on about?"

I shrugged. Queeg was using veiled speech intended to confuse the enemy. Instead, it was confusing us.

"Clarify Bravo or Golf persons," Greg demanded.

"I say again Bravo or Golf persons!" Queeg's voice whistled in our ears.

Greg looked at me. "This is like talking to a parrot."

Then it struck me: Bravo and Golf — the letters B and G. Black or grey. Black for Viet Cong uniforms, grey for North Vietnamese. I told Greg. He rolled his eyes in exasperation. Identifying a hidden enemy at night from two thousand feet was impossible.

Greg thumbed his transmit button. "We can't confirm Bravo-Golf."

"It's vital you confirm Bravo-Golf," Queeg replied in a deep voice.

I picture Queeg gazing steely-eyed at his map. This was his big chance. If we found the North Vietnamese regiment on its way to Nui Dat he'd appear on the ball to those in high places who mattered. Trumpets would blow and we'd all march past his Queegness in review order: *Heil to the saviour of the Task Force!*

He was dreaming. We knew the NVA wouldn't compromise their location by shooting at us. The bad guys below were small potatoes, probably a VC squad juiced up on rice wine, out for some fun. Obviously Queeg was hoping for a regiment marching shoulder to shoulder down the highway. *Hi Ho, Hi Ho, it's off to work we go* . . .

Queeg continued: "Sunray requires confirmation Bravo-Golf."

Sunray was the buzz-word for the Task Force commander.

Seems Queeg was performing before a high-powered audience, which accounted for the sudden drop in the tone of his voice: his way of displaying coolness under pressure.

"What now?" I asked Greg.

He looked at me blank-faced. "Nothing much we can do." He nodded at the wing tubes. "Except the rockets."

We had four rockets with five-kilo warheads. They packed a wallop similar to an artillery shell. Problem was, there were no sights fitted to the aircraft — a grease pencilled cross on the inside of the windshield was all the system could provide.

We banked around and approached the ruins from the east. Again the green tracer floated up, but this time it was way off-target. It passed below and north of us by at least a hundred metres. From their spacing we estimated the tracer was a heavy machine gun, probably 12.7mm. Definitely enemy. Apart from the fact that we were being shot at, they were using green tracer, which indicated Soviet or Chinese manufacture. Our tracer was red.

An odd combination, I remember thinking. The Commies use green and we use red. Shouldn't it be the other way round? Maybe swapping ammunition could be put on the agenda for the Paris Peace Talks instead of haggling over the shape of the conference table.

"It's coming from the temple," I called as I pinpointed the next burst. As they rattled past I reminded myself that between each tracer bullet were five rounds without tracer.

"One-four report!" Queeg called.

"Stand by," Greg replied. "We're making another run now."

A burst arced towards us. I counted the rounds. Five bright lights snapped overhead. They were probably firing at the sound of the engine — or maybe they had a starscope too. That was a disturbing thought. I dismissed it, but the next burst squirted even closer, passing a few metres under the starboard wing.

Greg reached out, lifted the cover on the arming switches, then eased the throttle. The nose dipped and the slipstream howled. The altimeter unwound: fifteen hundred, one thousand feet. Greg thumbed the fire button. Two rockets sizzled away, dwindling to twin points of light floating against the black. They hit fifty metres short of the temple ruins, blasting showers of red sparks high into the air.

As Greg pulled from the dive the tracer followed us again. Persistent buggers, I remember thinking. I focused the scope on the temple ruins but could see nothing but overgrown rubble. We levelled at a thousand feet and turned for another run.

Once again we dropped. Greg sent our last two rockets scorching twenty metres over the target. We banked away as the sound of the explosions reached us. "That'll put them off their stroke," Greg remarked as we levelled to take another look.

It must have discouraged them because the firing stopped. We weren't naive enough to think we'd caused any damage, but the VC didn't know we were out of rockets. Now they'd revealed their position the gun crew was probably bugging out. But how many were there? One gun crew at least — two, maybe three men. Hardly the regiment we were looking for. I scanned the area with the scope. All I could see were dozens of glowing patches where rocket fragments had set fire to dry grass.

"One-Four, report!" Queeg demanded.

"Cannot identify," Greg replied. "There's no sign of the enemy. I suggest we've only got a few men here."

"Maintain surveillance," Task Force replied.

"Maintain surveillance," Greg mimicked. "Shit, if we fly around in circles any longer we'll vanish up our own fundament."

We circled for another ten minutes. We drifted closer, dropped down to five hundred feet, but the VC remainded hidden and didn't fire at us. No amount of sticking our heads above the trench could evoke a response.

"Maybe it was a diversion," I suggested as we climbed away from a run over the temple. "Keep us occupied while something else is going on." But what, and where?

"Maybe," Greg replied. "Anyway, I've had enough of this shit. We're low on fuel. I'll make one more pass then we're heading back." He dropped the nose.

I checked the area but still could see any sign of movement. As we passed low over the ruins for the last time, the tracer suddenly flashed up again. This time it didn't miss.

VUNG TAU

Sergeant Bucknell left the 23rd Evac at 2000hrs. The Yanks were smart, he ruefully admitted, they'd secured a deal that promised to make everyone happy.

"There will be expenses," Bucknell had warned. "I can't get eight girls without money up front."

"How much do you need?" Ferraro asked.

Bucknell had organised several medium-sized orgies during his first tour. The going price then for take-away pussy was twenty dollars a head. That was eighteen months ago. Allowing for inflation caused mainly by American largesse he figured thirty dollars would get what he wanted.

Ferraro put it to his men. They overwhelmingly agreed. However, Ferraro suggested they all contribute fifty a head. He smiled at Bucknell. "When you come back with the goods, providing they're quality merchandise, you get to keep the difference plus the table stakes. That's eight hundred bucks to work with. You should be able to show a nice profit."

Bucknell didn't argue. Eight hundred dollars was two months pay. His night in Madame Vinh's would have to take a raincheck but there were other places where he knew he could get the goods at a reasonable price and still show a healthy profit.

With two hundred dollars for use as a down payment he set off. First stop was back to the Australian Hospital. Here he checked the orderly room. There was the usual duty NCO, a corporal, minding the phones with his nose buried in a *Playboy* magazine.

"How can I get the use of a vehicle?" Bucknell asked.

The NCO kept his nose in the centrefold. He shook his head. "You can't, Sarge. Anyway what do you want one for?"

"To get into Vung Tau — shit, it's only a few minutes drive."

"I can't authorise use of the duty vehicle."

"Who can, then?"

"Duty Sergeant. His name's Baxter. You'll find him down the hall, first office on the right."

Bucknell headed for the office. He found Baxter sitting with his boots on a desk, watching *McHale's Navy* on Armed Forces Television.

"What's it cost to get hold of a vehicle to go into Vung Tau?" Bucknell asked. He felt happier dealing with someone of his own rank. Things needed less explanation.

"What for?"

"A blow job."

"Mate, wait until tomorrow. There's a curfew here in two hours."

"There's twenty bucks in it for you."

Baxter raised his eyebrows. "How long do you need the vehicle for?"

"Quick trip to the Grand Hotel, then across to the 23rd Evac. The vehicle can either stay or come back here and do the return trip a few hours later."

"What in fuck are you organising?"

"Just say I've some Yank friends who need their tubes cleared."

"How many Yank friends?"

"Eight."

"Eight! Shit, you mean you're going to smuggle eight whores into the 23rd?"

"Well I can't take four and make them double up, can I? It wouldn't be hygienic."

Baxter smiled. "You expect me to assign you one of our duty vehicles?"

"One of those landrover ambulances would be perfect. Eight girls can fit in the back. The Yanks will let it into their compound without any questions. And with an ambulance we don't have to worry about the curfew."

"It's still risky."

"Look, we put the girls on the stretchers and cover them with blankets. Someone sits in the back with all the gear set up. Make it look as if we're transferring a few patients."

"You're nuts!"

"Okay, there's fifty bucks in it for you."

Baxter shook his head slowly. "I could lose my stripes over this."

"Okay then, make it a hundred."

"I'll get someone to stand in for me and be right with you." Baxter reached for the phone.

They stand on the runway, they rant, scream and shout,
'Bout lots of things they know fuck all about.
For the good that they're doing they might as well be
Shovelling shit on the Isle of Capri.

Forty thousand feet over the Pacific Ocean, the formation of six B-52s enroute from Guam to Vietnam was ahead of schedule. They'd picked up an unexpected jetstream that increased their groundspeed by almost a hundred knots.

"ETA over target is now 2115hrs," the lead navigator reported to the aircraft's captain.

"Shit, that's almost an hour early," the commander replied. "Better advise Ubon. Give them an updated flight refuelling time for the outbound leg while you're at it."

The navigator made his calculations, then, using his coded link SSB radio, spoke with Ubon airbase in Thailand. They acknowledged the amended Time Over Target and passed the new timings for flight refuelling to the KC-135 tanker squadron.

From Ubon a chain reaction of commands was set in motion. A coded message flashed via satellite link to MACV HQ Saigon, advising the mission would be early. At MACV the duty officer checked the decoded message then ordered the information passed on to the Air Traffic Control Centre at Tan Son Nhut airport. Code-named "Paris", the ATC centre was responsible for keeping aircraft clear of the safety zone surrounding the B-52s' target. They forwarded the information by teleprinter to the Australian Task Force Headquarters at Nui Dat.

The new strike timings were received and the Task Force HQ master map updated. As the new timings fell within the original time frame, allowing an hour's margin either side of the original strike estimate, no urgency was placed on passing the information farther down the line. The only aircraft operating in the Province that night were 161's two reconnaissance aircraft and they were briefed to remain clear of the area. However, the Task Force Duty Officer realised that 161 should be informed and ordered the new timings passed on to their Command Post. In one of those coincidences of war, just as the duty operator was about to pick up his direct line to Possum Control, the radio crackled with an urgent message.

It was Possum One-Four. The aircraft had been hit by ground fire and was returning to Nui Dat.

Possum One-Four

Ned Kelly

As the tracers reached towards us, Greg rammed the throttle open and kicked the Cessna around in a climbing turn. His actions probably saved a direct hit on the cockpit — I swear those green balls of light had my name on them. Rounds clanged into the engine, zipped past the cockpit, then stitched the fuselage with a staccato hammering. Holes magically appeared in the underside of the wing a few feet from my head. I held my breath, waiting for the aircraft to disintegrate around us.

White smoke poured from the instrument panel. I could smell burning electrical wiring. The smoke stung our eyes and filled the cabin despite the open door. I realised Greg was having difficulty seeing the instruments. The circuit breakers had popped, killing the panel lighting. He was learning forward, eyes glued to the artificial horizon. He made a quick radio call to Task Force, received an acknowledgment then pulled the master electrics switch. The smoke stopped and the cockpit cleared.

Greg's eyes were still on the artificial horizon. He eased the throttle then nudged the rudder pedals. Response was normal: the hits aft had missed the control cables. He pulled a pencil torch from his sleeve pocket and flashed it on the instruments. We were flying at about a thousand feet and climbing slowly. Engine boost, tacho and oil pressure were normal. The remaining instruments were dead. It was a miracle the engine was still running — I'd heard and felt at least three hits up front.

"A bullet must've shorted the power harness," Greg yelled

over the growl of the engine. Without power the intercom was useless. He handed me the torch, then pointed at the gyro compass. I directed the torch beam. The indicator was on 220^0 — almost the direct heading for Nui Dat.

Greg pushed the throttle open, squeezing as much power as he dared. I kept the torch on the instruments, searching for any sign of distress from the pounding engine. I prayed that the assembly line staff at Continental Aviation had been particularly vigilant when they'd bolted this engine together. Now was definitely not the time to find we had Monday's child turning the fan.

The engine throbbed steadily. We breathed easier. It was impossible to assess the damage while flying. I'd heard stories of World War Two aircraft being shot full of holes and pressing on to their target regardless. This wasn't WW2, I told myself. And this was a single-engined Cessna 180, a civil aircraft that had been modified for military use. It wasn't a four-engined Lancaster or B-17, it was a fragile collection of aluminium and rivets, not intended to be shot full of holes. *It was the cheapest aircraft the fucking government could buy!*

I glanced at the starboard wing. A glistening slick trailed from two holes. "We're losing fuel!" I yelled.

Greg tapped the fuel gauge. I aimed the torch. Part of the drill while on recon was to alternate fuel tanks hourly. We'd been using the port tank for the last hour, leaving what remained starboard as a reserve. But without power the gauges were lifeless. All we knew was that very little remained in the port tank and our starboard reserve was drenching Phuoc Tuy Province. The Cessna's fuel system didn't include a cross feed pump, so we couldn't save what remained by transferring fuel from the damaged tank. This was war on the cheap. For the want of a fifty dollar pump we could soon drop into the jungle and be gobbled up by angry VC. I wished I was a grunt back at Nui Dat — or even out on patrol. I'd have both feet on the ground and a fighting chance. But if the engine quit our chances over thick jungle were zero.

Greg switched tanks to simultaneous feed. At least we could use some of the fuel before it drained away. "Shine the torch on the magnetic compass!" he called suddenly.

I realised he was trying to fix our position. We'd been expecting the glow from the lights of Vung Tau to be visible at any moment, but they weren't there. I played the torch's thin beam on the compass at the top of the windshield. According to the compass we were heading roughly north-east. We were flying *away* from Nui Dat, not towards it.

"The gyro compass must be out!" Greg shouted. "Check it again!"

I swung the torch. The gyro was still reading south-west, almost 180^0 opposite the direction indicated by the magnetic compass.

Greg banked gently left, his eye on the luminous dial of the magnetic compass. It swung as we turned. I shone the torch on the gyro. It remained pointing south-west. I tried to reset it but the knob was jammed. As Greg levelled the wings we could see the glow from the lights of Vung Tau above the nose.

I checked the clock. We'd been flying in the wrong direction for almost five minutes. That was ten minutes worth of valuable fuel by the time we retraced our route.

Greg examined his map and made a quick calculation. "That puts us right in the middle of the restricted zone!" he called. "Lucky the strike's not due for another hour."

I nodded. Being caught in an Arc Light strike would be the last straw. My heart was thumping and I was drenched in sweat. It seemed an eternity since we'd been hit. I checked the engine gauges. Those still functioning remained steady. The Continental ran with a comforting beat from its six cylinders. Apart from the electrical and gyro compass damage, everything was functioning normally. I willed the engine to keep going.

We were at two thousand feet. The ground was shrouded in black. The void seemed hostile, like a hungry mouth waiting to swallow us. I couldn't suppress the nagging feeling that the bullets had done more damage. Maybe the control cables had been nicked and were inexorably twanging apart, strand by strand until one straining thread was all that stood between life and death. I wondered if I had a parachute, would I bail out? Definitely not, I concluded. Not yet, anyway. I glanced at the wing. The fuel leak had stopped, whether because the tank was empty or its rubber bladder had sealed, I couldn't tell. I wondered how far we could glide.

I cursed my overactive imagination. We'd be safely on the ground at Nui Dat in fifteen minutes or so. With luck the aircraft would be unserviceable for the rest of the night and we'd have to forego the next sortie. I could sneak a few cans of beer from the mess refrigerator than sit in the dark in my weapon pit and drink myself into oblivion. I could forget all about this stupid fucking place, about Queeg and bureaucrats who refused to give us the equipment we needed . . .

My thoughts were interrupted by a flash of light. I looked out of the door to see a rolling carpet of explosions sweeping towards us. There was no sound. Each explosion lit the jungle, casting flickering images of erupting earth and trees like a scene from an old time movie. As the first shockwaves slammed us I realised what it was.

"The B-52 strike!" I shouted.

My words were swamped by a wave of thunder. I remember thinking: *Shit, we're dead!*

NUI DAT

Waiting for the action to begin is probably the hardest part of any war. Around Nui Dat almost two thousand men had been waiting since sunset for signs of the enemy. After nightfall there had been alerts around the peerimeter, mostly animals hitting the barbed wire or tripping flares. The soldiers in the forward pits were used to this and weren't tempted into a hasty response. They knew the VC would love them to be spooked into opening fire. That would pinpoint the front positions — particularly those of the machine guns. That's where the VC's mortars and rockets would be aimed first. So they waited patiently, peering out into the cleared area surrounding the base and wondering just who was looking back from the jungle's fringe a kilometre away.

161 Recce Flight's perimeter abutted a battalion area on the northern side, so the chances of a breakthrough there were slim. It was the southern perimeter adjoining the airstrip that was the most exposed. Accordingly, strong points, roofed over with cor-

rugated iron and covered by sandbags, had been built at regular intervals. To cover a gap in the defences created by the runway's jutting finger, 161 Flight had been provided with a 105mm howitzer. If the screaming hoards did break through and came storming up the runway, the gun's Splintex rounds would make short work of them. That was the theory.

So far, the gun crew and those on alert along the airfield had seen nothing significant. The rubbish tip was smouldering and occasionally flames sparked into life, casting dancing shadows across the bitumen. To those watching, every shadow wore a conical hat and carried an AK-47.

Shortly before 2100hrs, a trail of fireflies, attracted by the flames, caused some apprehension. In the cloying darkness they glowed like candles, impossibly bright for such tiny insects. The gun crew swore they could see VC tiptoeing around the flames and were all for putting a round into the tip. The Gun layer cranked the gun towards the target.

The Squadron Sergeant Major soon put an end to their speculation: "Do you really think the fuckin' VC are going to sneak in like Wee Willy Winky with fuckin' candles, then fuck about in the fuckin' rubbish tip stealing mess scraps? The fuckin' cooking round here isn't *that* fuckin' good!"

No one could argue with such eloquent logic. The insects' fiery mating dance soon identified them. The gun crew relaxed and resighted the gun on its original line of fire. Everyone settled back into the tedious routine of waiting.

In 161's command post there was sudden tension of a different kind. Task Force HQ phoned through, advising of One-Four's last radio call. A fire on board an aircraft was one of the most terrifying incidents the crew could face, but there was very little anyone could do to help.

161's Sioux helicopters could react quickly but they weren't capable of winching the crew from the jungle, and being unarmed, they couldn't provide immediate protection. What was needed were Hueys based at Nui Dat to provide a rescue capability. Unfortunately, RAAF operational policy prevented such a commonsense precaution. They refused to leave aircraft with the Task Force overnight, claiming they could react to an emergency promptly from Vung Tau, thirty kilometres away.

In situations such as the crew of Possum One-Four now found themselves, time was critical. If they were forced down and survived the crash into the jungle without injury, their problems would only be starting. Experience had shown that helicopters as large as a tandem rotor Chinook could thrash through the jungle canopy yet leave little sign of its passage: a small Cessna could expect to be swallowed up without a trace. Even if the crew's emergency beacons worked, extracting them at night could still be a problem. And as the jungle was the VC's backyard, their survival time on the ground was anyone's guess.

161 did what little they could to assist. The chopper on recon east was diverted and another Cessna scrambled, the aim being to escort One-Four back. If One-Four did go in, the two aircraft would keep the area under surveillance until help arrived. The departing Cessna was delayed five minutes while the flarepath was lit. Once airborne it climbed with navigation and landing lights on. With One-Four's radios dead, the lights would assist the returning aircraft and also help to avoid a mid-air collision. It could also draw ground fire — a risk that had to be taken.

When news of One-Four's plight was passed down the line even those who were resting stirred from their tents. Everyone waited impatiently for the sound of an approaching engine.

VUNG TAU. L'HOTEL GRANDE

It was almost 2100hrs that balmy February evening when an Australian landrover ambulance wheeled into the courtyard of Vung Tau's Hotel Grande. A tall Australian Sergeant eased from the passenger's side, spoke briefly with the driver, then climbed the broad marble stairs into the hotel's entrance.

"Ha! Look who's returned!" A tall slim woman wearing a slinky jade green dress with slits running from calves to hourglass waist, oozed towards the soldier as he strode into the dimly lit foyer.

"I'll be buggered," Sergeant Bucknell squinted through the shadows. "Li! Are *you* still working here?"

"Of course, *mon chère* — business is too good to leave," Li purred, running the tip of her tongue along moist red lips. She pointed a manicured finger at a tag pinned on her left breast. It said: *Li, Hostess No. 1.* "This is a classy joint. I'm now Numbah One girl. Plenty important."

Bucknell smiled. He glanced around at the shabby walls and smoke-stained ceilings. Somewhere in the distance he could hear the urgent throb of disco music. "Sure, darling. The place hasn't changed a bit."

L'Hotel Grande was the biggest dive in Vung Tau. Once the old hotel by the sea had been a miniature Versailles Palace, boasting soaring marble columns, elegant fountains, crystal chandeliers and frescoed ceilings, as many of the trappings of nineteenth century France as the original owners could cram between its stone walls. Its heyday was in the 1920s, when Vung Tau had been a holiday Mecca favoured by wealthy plantation owners and bureaucrats — whose indulgences sowed the seeds of revolution among the Vietnamese.

The hotel fronted a wide boulevard that skirted a palm-fringed beach. During the day the tropical heat was tempered by a gentle sea breeze. Smiling street vendors, carefully policed by the French authorities, sold fresh fruit from the orchards and seafood from the fishing fleet that worked the teeming coastal waters around Cape St Jacques. A favourite tourist pastime used to consist of watching the fishing fleet land the afternoon catch, bidding for live lobsters and shrimps, then having them prepared by the hotel's team of Cordon Bleu chefs. In the evening the hotel guests could promenade along the brightly lit beach front secure in the knowledge that they were safe here as on the Champs Elysees.

L'Hotel Grande became a glittering attraction for wealthy international tourists. Cruise liners called at the port of Vung Tau, their passengers taking guided tours to see the hotel and to witness for themsleves the benevolence of French colonialism. Meanwhile, ten kilometres inland, the rice farmers were taxed until they starved.

During the Second World War, the hotel was taken over by

the Japanese to house high-ranking officers. After the war it struggled vainly to regain its former glory, becoming a favoured haunt of French officers on leave during the subsequent Indo-China war. After the French surrender in 1954, it was all downhill for the gem of the South China Sea coast. By the sixties, the hotel had decayed into a seething bordello. Stripped of its former elegance by a succession of pillaging occupiers, its paint was flaking and most of the delicate frescoes had vanished beneath layers of grime. Oddly enough, the flushing toilets still worked and the spotlit fountains in the courtyards continued spouting, recalling echoes of former splendour.

During the Vietnam war the hotel was leased by the Australian and American Army as a leave centre. Pimps and prostitutes prowled grounds and bars once frequented by the ladies and gentlemen of French society. Even the name had been bastardised. It was now "The Grand", pronounced in a coarse Australian accent that would make a French elocution teacher swoon with despair.

As Sergeant Bucknell's eyes adjusted to the dim light he peered down Li's magnificent cleavage. "My, you've certainly come up in the world," he said.

"Help from an American Navy doctor." Li smiled and pushed her breasts forward. "He horny devil too. I give plenty Boom Boom, he give me tits like film star."

Even without artificial endowment Li would have been a beautiful woman. Of French-Vietnamese parents, she was the result of a genetic combination that took the best from both races to produce a tall, Eurasian vixen who caught every man's eye. Such a goddess was known among soldiers as a "Frenchy", a highly desirable creature who could demand (and get) more than twice the price of the ordinary street girl.

Bucknell had met her during his first tour in '65. She'd worked in a bar at Ben Hoa airbase frequented by the Australians. When the Australians redeployed to Phuoc Tuy Province and established their base at Nui Dat, Li and some of her bargirl friends followed, getting work at the Vung Tau Grand where they knew their Australian clientele would soon appear. This had struck Bucknell as a little odd when he discovered her there a few weeks later. The Australians had established a reputation amongst Vietnamese whores as being Cheap Charlies — partly because of their reluctance to pay for sex, but mainly due to the fact they weren't as highly paid as the free spending Americans. So for Li to follow the Australians didn't make economic sense.

However, soldiers are capable of extraordinary rationalisation. For Li and Co to prefer to associate with them rather than the wealthy Americans was a tribute to Aussie bed prowess — so they theorised. However, the Battalion's Intelligence Officer soon deflated their egos. The explanation was that Li and her girls were known VC agents. Rather than a new batch of girls having to win the Aussies' confidence all over again, what better way to keep the information flowing than by installing familiar faces (and rear ends) in Vung Tau. And what better way to feed the VC false information than by letting them operate unhindered. It was a cosy little arrangement that fooled no one, but as the Int Officer put it, made the job of counter espionage "great sport but rather exhausting".

Li kissed Bucknell on the cheek. She slid her arm into his and led him down a long dark corridor towards the source of the pounding music. In the distance a slit of red light seeped from beneath a closed door, casting shadows on two Vietnamese men lurking either side of the entrance. Bucknell hesitated, but Li reassured him with a whisper in his ear followed by a hot moist tongue that sent urgent shivers up his spine. One of the men stepped forward and pushed the door open. Li led the way. Light and disco music exploded around them as they entered a ballroom that had once echoed to Viennese waltzes but now shook to the beat of *Good Vibrations*.

Australian and American soldiers clutched girls in sweaty embraces. Others crowded a bar patrolled by harlots bursting the seams of their satin dresses. A Vietnamese Presley-clone wearing aviator sunglasses sat on a podium behind a mountain of audio equipment. Like a battlefield general he sought out potential clients and directed girls with the skill of a stockmarket operator.

Li led the way across the surging dance floor to a corner alcove surrounded by plastic palm trees. They entered, followed by inquisitive stares from other clients. She drew a beaded curtain behind her.

"You still got all your friends here?" Bucknell asked. From similar alcoves nearby he could hear the thrashings and gruntings of mercenary sex.

"Most of them, but I have *bookoo* new girls," Li replied as they eased into a soft velvet seat. She spoke in the colloquial blend of French, English and Vietnamese that was the verbal currency of the war. "Now can I show you good time, or are you tired of me?" She feigned a sad expression while slipping her hand to Bucknell's thigh and massaging gently. "I hope you still want Li — even though I am Number One girl we can have lots of fun. Just like we did before. Plenty Boom-Boom. I give you one in four free or twenty-five per cent discount."

"That's what I like about you, darling — your sincerity." Bucknell's voice croaked. He could feel his groin stirring. Li's perfume was subtle, unlike the cheap rose-scented toilet water used by most of the Vung Tau whores. "I need some of your girls."

"Oh, how many you want?"

Bucknell was feeling lightheaded. The throbbing music, the perfume and Li's warmth had drained the blood from his brain, sending it pumping to his thighs. He was becoming tumescent, certain that any moment his penis was going to burst up the front of his shirt like a striking cobra. He forced himself to concentrate on the business at hand. "I need eight girls for the night."

"Eight! Xa! Bucky, you *are* horny — just like old times." Li exclaimed as her fingers deftly worked his trouser buttons.

"They're not for me. They're for my friends."

"That good. You save yourself for me." Li smiled. "You want scrubbers or quality stuff?"

"Only the best. Tight — and clean."

"For you I can do." Li recoiled in mock surprise as his flies sprang apart and his eagerness was revealed. Her hand burrowed inside like a little animal seeking warmth. "Now let us negotiate price — say sixty dollars per girl."

Bucknell later described the negotiations as the most difficult bargaining session of his life. "It's almost impossible to talk sense with a woman like Li hanging on to your stalk. She was moving her hand back and forth in a delicious rhythm. I'd shake my head and say forty dollars — so she'd slow the motion. She'd then demand fifty-five and speed up again. I'd say forty-five and she'd slow. In between bids she was asking me questions about my wife and kids, had I seen so and so from the old battalion — oh, and by the way, how was the *new* battalion.

I knew she was doing her bit for the cause and she knew I knew. But we played the game anyway. Because, it was more fun than bamboo slivers under the fingernails. My answers were vague. I must've made about as much sense as an Australian politician talking economics — the only difference being that when *they* talk it's their own hand doing the stroking.

Eventually we settled on fifty dollars per girl, two hundred immediately with the balance to be paid on completion of mission. Li sealed the contract by dropping her head into my lap and going to work. I remember sighing and looking up at the ceiling to see a faded pink cherub on a cloudy background staring inquisitively down at me. I wondered what the little bare-arsed voyeur thought of the scenes he'd witnessed during the years he'd been perched up there . . ."

After Li administered the *coupe de grâce*, Bucknell ordered a beer. Li spoke to one of her girls and a few minutes later there were eight primping harlots lined up for inspection. Bucknell looked them over quickly then nodded approval. They were whisked outside and loaded into the ambulance.

Bucknell drained his beer then followed reluctantly, armed with a promise that when he returned Li would give him a brain shattering freebie with all the trimmings. The ambulance clashed gears and sped back through the night towards the 23rd Evac.

At about the same time, forty kilometres north, Possum One-four was battling for its life.

Yea though I walk through the valley of the shadow of death I will fear no evil

Ned Kelly

"Whoever wrote the twenty-third psalm had never been caught in a B-52 bombing raid. I was frightened witless. Bombs were raining down all around. Any moment one of them would hit the aircraft and vaporise us. My final thoughts would become fading electrical impulses drifting on the ether, perhaps to be picked up as a scratch of static on some Vietnamese peasant's transistor radio. Or worse, maybe I'd be reincarnated as a Viet Cong and spend my new life eating rice and fish heads while being hunted by my former mates.

I don't care what anyone says about the moment of death; about great calm, tunnels of light or even the past parading across the mind's screen like a *M.A.S.H.* re-run. None of this happened to me. But then I didn't die, so maybe my observations don't qualify. What *did* happen was everything snapped into slow motion as terror generated a flood of adrenalin which swamped my brain.

The explosions became huge red flowers opening their petals. I saw falling bombs, frozen mid-air by the stroboscopic effect of preceding impacts. Debris freeze-framed into the sky, trees were plucked from the ground and shredded. For a moment I thought fragments were reaching up to us, for they were level with the wingtip. Then I realised it was the aircraft; we were rolled — no, *flipped* — inverted.

In my fright I dropped the starscope. It fell out of the door and tumbled away into the night. All I could do was hang on in terror and silently mouth the words "Oh shit!" over and over again.

How the aircraft was missed by more than four hundred bombs is one of those fortuitous flukes that old soldiers dine out on for the rest of their lives.

Greg McBride

"All I knew was that the cockpit was suddenly filled with light. Then there was a rumbling sound, a giant, continuous explosion that seemed to thicken the air and squeeze the breath from my lungs. I was looking ahead of the aircraft at the glow from Vung Tau when the shock wave hit us. The smudge of light whipped to the top of the windshield. We rolled — something the Cessna wasn't built for. I remember thinking quite calmly: the wings are going to snap off.

When I realised they were still intact, I hung onto the yoke and tried to regain control. I couldn't see the artificial horizon, the only reference I had was the glow of Vung Tau's lights on the horizon. As they approached their correct position I applied opposite aileron. But they kept on going. At the same time the aircraft was being hammered by shock waves. It was like being inside an oil drum rolling down a hill with someone belting it with a sledgehammer.

I think we did two, maybe three, revolutions, I'll never know for sure. In a few seconds the explosions had swept past us. I levelled the wings and kept the nose pointing towards the glow on the horizon. We'd lost about a thousand feet in altitude and were pretty shaken but otherwise okay. I think we owe our lives to the lights of Vung Tau; without them, there was no way I could have kept orientation as we were tossed around."

Ned Kelly

After the explosions rolled past, I found myself staring at the glow from the lights of Vung Tau. I felt unusually elated. For a moment I thought: *maybe I'm dead* — everything seemed so calm and peaceful. Then I saw a huge light in the sky, ahead and above, approaching fast. It was surrounded by a shimmering silver halo, tinged with red and green. I thought: *So this is it — St Peter's come to fetch us. At least it's not the guy with horns and red tuxedo.*

Light filled the cockpit. The sound of our engine and slipstream seeped back into my ears. I saw a shadow behind the light then realised it was another aircraft. It banked around and dropped into formation ten metres off the port wing. I could see the pilot and observer in the cockpit. They waved and gave us a thumbs-up. I could've kissed them.

❖ ❖

Ten minutes later Possum One-Four, escorted by One-Five, landed at Nui Dat. One-Four shut down near the refuelling point and the crew climbed shakily from the aircraft. After a quick check with a shaded torch they found five bullet holes in the engine compartment. Four had passed through the side of the cowling, two glancing off the cylinder cooling fins and two missing the engine entirely. The fifth had ripped through a power harness near the cabin firewall. Seven other bullets hit along the fuselage, one grooving across the back of the observer's then the pilot's seat before exiting through the cabin roof. The rest stitched evenly along the fuselage to the tail, missing the control cables by inches. A torch under the instrument panel soon revealed the cause of the faulty directional gyro. A shard of metal, chipped off the engine by a bullet, had drilled through the instrument's case and wedged the compass ring. It was a fluke that almost cost two men's lives.

The ground crew hitched the aircraft to a landrover and towed it to the hangar, where the damage could be fully assessed under lights. The aircraft's crew headed for the CP. Both men were subdued and wide-eyed. They couldn't believe their luck. Apart from the bullet holes, no one, to their knowledge, had ever flown through two hundred tons of falling explosive and lived to tell about it. Little did they know there was yet another surprise in store for them.

Ned Kelly

Naturally, everyone was relieved that we'd made it back safely. We gave a quick rundown of what happened. The ground fire was really no big deal — our aircraft were always taking hits — but twelve hits was some kind of record. Greg gave a graphic description accompanied by hand maoeuvres that made it appear as if a battery of AAA had us in their sights (which wasn't far from the truth). The climax was a masterpiece of mimicry with Greg's eyes afire as he described how it felt to fly through the middle of a B-52 raid *and survive*.

The Engo appeared as Greg finished. His face was grim. The aircraft was suffering from an extreme case of sprung rivets. It seemed that the fuselage and wings had been in the process of literally unzipping. "Just a little more stress and the whole aircraft would have let go," the Engo groaned. "The only thing holding it together was the paint!"

I suspected he was exaggerating but I was in no mood to challenge him.

Dave Brown had checked with Task Force and found there'd been new strike timings passed down from MACV. However, the timings had reached Task Force HQ at about the same time as the strike was going in. Although we had a valid reason for improving the procedures for passing on information, there was no point in creating a witch hunt over the incident. If we hadn't strayed into the restricted area there would not have been a problem, even if the strike *was* early. In the confusion after the bullets hit, Greg was more concerned about the cockpit fire than anything else. The damaged gyro compass and circumstances conspired against us to do the rest.

While we were discussing our luck, the phone from Task Force HQ jangled. Sergeant Brown took the call. He spoke briefly then looked at me as if he'd been slapped across the face with a dead mullet. He offered the phone with his hand over the mouthpiece: "It's Cap'n Queeg, sir. You better take this."

I took the receiver. "Yessir?" I said apprehensively. Surely Queeg was only phoning us to express his relief that we were okay. Maybe the little prick was going to congratulate us on a job well done. That would be a first.

"Lieutenant!" Queeg launched in a pompous tone. "I've noted the timings of Possum One-Four's last radio call . . ."

I realised he wasn't aware that I'd been on board the aircraft, nor that we'd been caught in the middle of the B-52 strike. It occurred to me if he did find out he'd try and use it against us. So I kept my mouth shut. I wasn't ready for what came next.

". . . the pilot reported, and I quote: 'We are twenty clicks north east of Nui Dat, electrical fire in cockpit, returning immediately, shutting down electrics.' Do you concur?"

"Sounds right," I answered, puzzled at what he was driving at. Quite honestly I couldn't remember what Greg's last radio call was, but I was sure it would've been words to that effect. I thought: Who gives a blue-arsed damn anyhow?

Queeg continued: "Now, I've calculated the time it takes a Cessna to fly that distance. It should have taken about nine or ten minutes depending on prevailing winds. Instead, it was almost twenty minutes until the aircraft landed! A ten minute difference — do you realise that's an error of one hundred per cent!"

My bomb-rattled brain couldn't believe what I was hearing. The little son-of-a-bitch was griping about ten minutes of lost time! While we were being blown around the sky like a hayseed in a cyclone, Queeg was playing armchair general! No doubt he'd been strutting around the Task Force command post, sticking pins in his map and brown-nosing to the senior staff. I felt my temper rising.

"Ten minutes Lieutenant, ten minutes!" Queeg shrieked. "What happened to those lost ten minutes?"

This can't be happening, I thought. If we were billing Task Force HQ for flight time by the minute and Queeg was a cost account, I could understand his concern. But this was supposed to be a war. The static on the line started to sound like the click of ball-bearings. I waited for him to cross-examine me about missing strawberries. One of us was definitely insane. I suspected it was Queeg.

"Now Lieutenant, you tell me," Queeg babbled in a high-pitched voice that sounded like a tin robot about to blow a fuse. "How is it possible for the pilot to make such a gross error of judgment. Can't he navigate, eh?"

I was momentarily struck dumb. Along with all the other nonsense we had to put up with, we now had a staff officer rowing around Task Force HQ with only one oar in the water.

"Answer me, Lieutenant, can't your pilot navigate?" Queeg bawled. "Tell me, eh? eh? *Tell meee!*"

So I told him, then hung up in his ear. I headed for the mess-hut where I found the movie grinding through its fourth reel. I sat down and watched Napoleon's retreat from Moscow.

VUNG TAU 2130HRS

Sergeant Bucknell had no problem smuggling his load of whores into the 23rd Evac hospital. Baxter drove boldly up to the gate and announced he was there to collect a patient. The two American soldiers on duty didn't give them a second look; an Australian accent and an Australian ambulance were credentials they couldn't argue with. They waved them through without checking. The vehicle slipped in and parked behind the recuperation ward.

"I'll make sure they're ready," Bucknell warned Baxter. He pointed to the light in the window. "I'll signal if everything's clear. Back up to it and unload. And f'Chrissake keep them quiet!" One of the girls had started giggling and the laughter was spreading.

Bucknell climbed out, made his way round to the front entrance and crept into the ward. The lights were low and fortunately the administrative area outside the section housing Ferraro and his men was deserted.

"Did you get them?" Ferraro asked as Bucknell pushed the door aside.

"They're outside." Bucknell checked around him. Only a small night lamp was burning at the far end of the room. Ferraro was still dressed in his uniform, the other seven were in bed. They all looked expectantly at Bucknell. Little sheet teepees rose in anticipation.

"Well, bring 'em in." Ferraro rubbed his hands eagerly. "We've only got an hour and a half before night rounds."

Sergeant Bucknell recalls that what followed is barely printable:

I helped the girls in through the window. Ferraro, like all good Sergeants, made sure his men were taken care of first. The girls were assigned without argument, until he took a liking to the third whore as she climbed in and kept her for himself. In a few minutes all the girls were in bed and the men were hammering away. Even the black man with the drip in his arm was at it, flat on his back with a tart astride him. She bobbed up and down, straight-backed, with a prim expression on her face that reminded me of a highborn lady cantering her pony at a country fair.

Ferraro was very gracious. When he found I hadn't brought a girl along for myself he offered me seconds. I declined, and told him I'd be fixed up later. (I didn't tell him about Li, I preferred to appear as the sacrificing ally.) Ferraro went to a bed locker, pulled out a bottle of Jack Daniels and tossed it to me. There was a spare bed in one corner of the ward, so, after sticking my head out of the window and telling Baxter to have the vehicle back in position at 2300hrs, I took off my shirt, poured myself a slug of Bourbon and lay on the bed.

For an hour unmentionable things happened. The culmination was a game of Bingo between four of the Americans who were capable of getting out of bed. Bingo is a disgusting depravity but hilarious to watch, particularly with half a bottle of bourbon under your belt. The four men arranged the beds in a rough square, two on either side of the ward, then on the word go everyone went at it.

The object of the game was that when any of the men felt they were nearing climax they shouted *Bingo*. Everyone then dismounted, moved to the girl on their right, saddled up and went at it again. After a while the shouts of *Bingo* became closer and the dismount-remount procedure became frenetic — and dangerous for the tardy. The girls seemed to love it all. Finally Ferraro called a halt. "Okay fellas, finish them off. Ten minutes before ward rounds!"

There was a final bout of thrashing and moaning from the beds. The girls then climbed from beneath the sheets and slipped into their clothing with the precision of a football cheer squad. They lined up under Sergeant Ferraro's guidance and were whisked through the window into the waiting ambulance.

I went to the window and told Baxter to collect me after he'd returned the girls to the Grand Hotel. He drove away, we shut the window and that was that. A perfect mission.

"Shit, that was *great!*" Ferraro said to me as he flopped on his bed and stared at the ceiling. There was a chorus of assent from the troops. I poured another drink and downed it. Then I passed out.

NUI DAT
Ned Kelly

The artillery battery south of the airfield punched six rounds over my tent. I snapped awake and lay on my bunk, listening to the freight-train rumble of 105mm shells as they flew out into the jungle. They exploded with hollow, rolling thumps, like the beating of distant drums. Once more I wondered who was dying.

Yet another day, I thought with some trepidation as I heard the clarion call of *"Gooooood morning, Vee-et-nam"* echo from radios in the tents around me.

"Fuck Vee-et-nam!" our soldiers' chorus replied.

I checked my watch. It was 0600hrs. I wasn't due on until 0700 — an extra hour as compensation for last night's late duty. I swung my feet to the floor and flicked on the lamp. I picked up a pencil and marked my calendar. Only 182 days to go! I had passed the halfway mark.

"At last!" I sighed. I was now on the downhill run. Australia was suddenly not quite so distant. Flushing toilets, long showers and acres of white pussy would soon be mine. I lay back, contemplating the things I missed. The first item that came to mind was fresh milk. I hadn't tasted fresh milk in six months. A tall, frosted glass swam before my eyes.

On the flight line a chopper spluttered into life. It was John Devlin setting out on the first light recon. He'd decided that lying around the tent for the next fourteen days was too boring to manage and had returned himself to duty. I listened while the engine smoothed to a steady rhythm then deepened to a growl as John applied pitch to the rotor blades. I could picture every movement he was making as the aircraft lifted to a hover, floated over the flight line, then dipped its nose and climbed away into the rising sun.

I grabbed my shaving gear and headed for the shower. The rubber plantation seemed friendlier, the light shafting between the trees somehow softer, less threatening. Maybe today it would rain, I thought. That would bring new problems: mud, drenching humidity and poor visibility for flying. But at least it would be a change from endless days of dry heat, dominated by a coppery sun that burned everything to a crisp. And the rubber trees would get new leaves. The thick shade would return. It would be *different!*

Armed Forces Radio was playing another Beatles tune. *Michele My Belle* drifted through the rubber. It seemed fitting. God was in his heaven and I was in the final stretch. And — I reminded myself — last night I'd bored it right up Queeg's arse. Score one-nil, my favour. There'd been nothing said about it since. I figured I'd temporarily spiked the little bugger's cannon. I was sadistically looking forward to crossing swords with him today.

It was 0645hrs when I arrived in the CP. Sergeant Brown was already on duty, his nose buried in a new motorbike magazine that came with yesterday's mail. His transistor radio was tuned to Armed Forces Radio, an episode of *Chicken Man* reaching its bizarre climax. Dave looked up.

"Any problems?" I asked.

"Only the usual reports from Task Force." He pointed to the row of clipboards with their freshly printed sheets.

I glanced through the Int summaries. MACV was still stacking bodies like cordwood . . .

"Task Force wanted us to assess last night's strike area," Dave continued. "They sent an Intelligence Officer along as observer on Lieutenant Devlin's first light recon."

The memory of the B-52 strike sent shivers up my spine. At least we'd hit them hard, I reflected. That would teach them to fuck with us.

The flight net radio suddenly crackled with John Devlin's voice. I picked up the handpiece: "Go ahead, Two-Three."

"Aah, just thought you'd like to know," John's voice vibrated. "I'm over the strike area now. Those bombs fell in a real tight pattern. Cleared the jungle for a click. Should make good farmland. Only problem is, the impact zone's five clicks short of the target."

"Shit!" I swore. I turned and looked at the map. The area was still marked in red. It seemed so big, so easy to hit — yet the B-52s, with all their electronic wizardry, had missed it by more than three miles. Three miles, after a flight of three thousand, represented an error of .05 per cent or, as MACV later claimed: "Arc Light sorties were 99.95 per cent accurate." So much for statistics.

I thought I heard an Asian voice giggling as John signed off. My imagination again. I tossed the handset aside and looked at Dave. *"C'est la guerre,"* he shrugged as he picked up the phone to pass on the news to the Task Force CP. I slumped in a chair and cursed the world. I'd been almost killed for no reason. That really deflated my ego.

"Task Force says we're to increase the recon schedule," Dave announced smugly after he'd put down the phone. "Give priority to the north-east."

"Here we go again," I muttered, gripped by an intense feeling of *déjà-vu*. I stared at the map, wondering what Charley was up to in those neat green squares. I pictured swarms of VC filtering through the jungle like ants. The definitive yellow horde yet again. I shuddered. To fire my growing depression, Armed Forces Radio introduced General Westmoreland with another of his morale boosters: "American soldiers and brave Allies," Westy began. "Let me tell you that your efforts and sacrifices during this treacherous Communist offensive . . ." Was there no escape from the simpering bastard? I glared at the transistor radio. Dave reached out and flicked it off as I fondled the butt of my pistol.

Another phone rang. It was our Quartermaster. He wanted me to fill out paperwork explaining the loss of the starscope.

"But QM, it wasn't Army property," I protested. "We traded the Americans six cases of beer and ten slouch hats for the bloody thing!"

"I know, zur," Shorrock replied. "But because we used hats-felt, khaki as part of the trade goods, I had to put the scope-star on our inventory. You have to fill out a loss and damage report so I can get it *off* the inventory."

"But it was lost due to enemy action!"

"I was told you dropped it out of the aircraft."

"Yes, but —" I realised my crime was not falling out with the scope. The paperwork would have been a lot simpler.

"Lookee, zur, I can write it off as due to enemy action.

Frankly, it doesn't worry me if you traded the bloody thing in Vung Tau for a bit o' nookie, har! har! Just sign on the dotted line, I'll take care of the rest. The system will issue us another."

"But our system doesn't have starscopes to issue!" I was getting angry. "That's why I traded slouch hats for the fucking thing in the first place!"

"You and I know that, but the system doesn't. You see, we're using wartime accounting. Once we've got a piece of equipment, its ours for the duration. If we lose it due enemy action, we can make an emergency requisition for replacement from the Yanks."

"Even though officially we haven't got it?"

"That's right, zur. It doesn't matter *how* we got it."

This was headlines to me. "But why in the first place didn't we pretend that we'd always had one, and then bullshit about losing it? It would've saved me collecting the money to pay for six cases of beer and all that haggling with the Yanks!"

"Zur, that wouldn't be honest," the QM reprimanded. "The system *knows* we didn't 'ave one in the first place."

"But . . . but . . ." I'd always known the Army's supply system was weird, but now it was bordering on the supernatural. Shorrock's explanation sounded like some kind of steady-state origins-of-the-universe theory. I pictured streams of military hardware materialising at the centre of the cosmos, drifting out to its edge then vanishing into black holes to be recycled.

"Now, zur, if you'll do the paperwork I'll have a new 'un in time for tonight's recons."

I realised I was cornered — yet another victory to our Welsh pirate. I agreed to fill out his damned Form Seven-Zero-Eight in triplicate. As I slowly lowered the phone I suppressed a strange urge to sing *Rule Britannia*.

Davie Brown looked at me. "I almost forgot," he announced cautiously. "There's a staff officer coming over from Task Force at 0900hrs to speak to you."

"Speak to me?" I shook my head. "You sure he wants me?"

"He asked specifically for you." Dave checked his note pad. "He's a major from the legal branch."

My heart sank. Legal! Surely they didn't want in on the starscope act too. "What the hell do they want?" I snapped.

"They didn't say," Dave warily replied. "But I reckon it's something to do with Cap'n Queeg."

Oh shit! That could only mean one thing. The little prick had made an official complaint after I told him off last night. "Jesus, Dave, are you sure?"

"Just a feeling," he shrugged.

Feeling? Voodoo was more like it. I knew Brown would've listened to the morning's jungle telegraph, those mystical vibes that permeated the shower block and dunnies at sunrise. I broke out in a cold sweat. Dave looked at me. "Do you reckon it's something to do with what you said to Cap'n Queeg?"

"That's what worries me," I replied. The Army loved punishing insubordinate junior officers. And there were few more junior or insubordinate than I.

"To make a case they need witnesses. I know nothing," Brown said. "I've already spread the word."

"Thanks," I replied. The knowledge that everyone would close ranks to protect their own was encouraging. I cursed Queeg. I knew it wasn't the done thing to abuse officers senior in rank, but he'd asked for it. If Queeg was a colonel or even a major I could understand the hierarchy getting its nose out of joint. But he was only a Captain — just a few notches higher than me. The big difference was, Queeg was a Duntroon graduate. They were the holiest of holies. They'd unite to protect their image, particularly as I was a six-month wonder. Justice would need to be seen to be done. My goose was as good as cooked.

But without witnesses Queeg was snookered! I decided that if I was questioned I'd deny any suggestion of insubordination. Let them try and make a case then! For a moment I felt confident, but then I remembered that the Army could do anything it wanted. Even if they couldn't prove my guilt they could make life miserable for me. Within a few days I'd be clumping around the jungle, rifle in hand. I wasn't cut out to be a grunt.

I slumped in a chair and brooded. This was the final straw. I thought we were here to fight the VC — not each other. Near the door our M-60 machine gun stood on its bipod, a belt of ammunition draped over the barrel, cartridges glinting in the sun. I contemplated the joy of storming over to Task Force HQ, kicking in the door to Queeg's kingdom and blowing him and his nest of petty bureaucrats away. Jesus! I thought. This place is getting to me. I'm crazier than Queeg. As I waited for the Lord High Executioner to arrive I tried to dismiss the rampaging image. But the more I thought about it, the more attractive it became.

I reached into my shirt pocket and retrieved last night's letter. I unfolded the crisp, perfumed paper and read her lines again. The words were reassuring, exactly what I'd wanted to hear after such a long wait. As I read I forgot all about Queeg and Vietnam. My sanity returned.

What am I doing here?

Mike Dawson

The crack of artillery ripping over my tent made me jump. How I was supposed to get used to it was beyond me. I'd hardly slept during the night. The new surroundings, the unfamiliar sounds, the heat and the threat of an enemy attack had kept me snapping awake every few minutes. Yet I could hear Ross Hutchinson snoring softly from the other side of the tent. His breathing hadn't even skipped a beat at the sound of the guns. I felt miserable, the excitement of yesterday having been well and truly dampened by reality.

I climbed from beneath the mosquito net. Today was my second day in country. Ross would be flying me around the Province, showing me the procedures, the layout of the area, the hundred and one things I had to learn before I could fly sorties alone.

I heard a chopper take off. The rising sun was casting a square of gold onto the tent's floor, giving promise of another hot day. I looked at the little calendar someone had thoughtfully pinned to the sandbag near the head of my bunk. At least now I only had three hundred and sixty *four* days to go. I'd already decided that I wasn't going to count the days — not yet anyway, the high numbers were too discouraging. When I got down to a hundred, then maybe I'd reconsider.

I looked around for my shaving gear, grabbed a towel and my rifle, then headed cautiously for the showers.

"Arise, Sir Knight, thou hast done well."

VUNG TAU

Sergeant Bucknell

I think I slept better that night than any other in Vietnam. Yesterday's combination of tension, the effects of the laxative overdose plus the subsequent sex and booze really knocked me out. When I woke I was momentarily disoriented. It took me a while to realise that I was still in the recuperation ward of the American 23rd Evac.

I blinked against the light and looked across to see Sergeant Ferraro propped up in his bed. He raised an urgent finger to his lips then nodded to the far end of the ward. I followed his gaze.

An American one-star General, resplendent in starched uniform, polished black helmet and pearl handled pistol low on his hip, was moving from bed to bed. He was followed by a Major clutching a briefcase. A movie cameraman and an assistant holding a tape recorder trailed close behind. The General paused at each bed, looked at the name on the patient's chart, then accepted a little purple box held out by the Major. He flipped the box open, placed it in the soldier's left hand, shook his right, then stepped back and snapped a salute. I heard him say something about: ". . . wounded in battle — I salute you."

I realised the General was handing out Purple Hearts. I watched, fascinated by his theatrics. More than once the cameraman asked for a retake. The General would rewind like a clockwork toy, then go through the routine again, complete with speech. I glanced at Ferraro, but he shook his head in one of those not-to-worry expressions. He mouthed something to me and half-closed his eyes. I got the message — act as if I was heavily sedated. I drooped my eyelids and through furry slits watched the General posture his way towards me.

After presenting Ferraro with the purple heart twice (the cameraman wanted an angled shot which showed the General's jut-jawed profile) the group stopped at the foot of my bed. The General looked at my chart. I realised that Ferraro must have written my name on the clipboard, because the General smiled and said: "Well done, Sergeant Bucknell, you're a true warrior!"

I fluttered my eyes and grunted. The General placed a purple heart on my bedside table then took a pace back. He sucked in his belly and his entire body seemed to inflate. His chin grew into a huge square block and the rest of his head vanished into his helmet. The camera whirred. The General threw a knife-edge salute. For a moment I feared he'd explode, but the camera stopped and the General safely deflated. The group turned as one then marched from the ward like a khaki centipede.

"Great work!" Ferraro called.

"Who was that?" I asked, watching the doors flap to and fro, concerned the General would suddenly wise up and return.

"He won the Congressional Medal in Korea. Now all the mother does is go round field hospitals presenting medals. I remembered late last night that he was due. So I filled in your chart — you're now a member of the Third Marine Battalion." He smiled broadly. "We haven't got a Third Battalion, by the way."

The men laughed. The black man with the drip in his arm called: "Hey, Aussie, how's it feel to be a jarhead?"

So that's why the General called me a warrior! It was a tradition of the Marine Corps — their commanders referred to marines as warriors in casualty reports. It was a touch Wagnerian but I liked its connotation. I could picture myself in Valhalla surrounded by buxom, eager women . . . I picked up the medal. It had been engraved with my name and rank. "But how —"

Ferrari said: "The General's aide made an inspection earlier this morning. He took your name and had the extra medal prepared — one of his staff carries spare medals and a portable engraver. They'll be in Ben Hoa in half an hour, doing the whole routine again for the camera.''

It was extraordinary. No doubt one day the American system would fail to match my name to the appropriate records and the Pentagon's computers would blow a fuse.

"I shouldn't really accept this." I fingered the medal. To me it was almost a sacred object. Unlike the Americans, our system is very lean on handing out awards. I'd been wounded on my first tour and spent two weeks in the Australian hospital after a mortar fragment had sliced my stomach. But our military doesn't award Purple Hearts.

Ferraro said: "We saw the scar. You've earned it."

So that was it. After I'd passed out they'd tucked me into bed. They would've seen the scar and assumed it was the wound I told them about as a pretext for being here. I thought about it for a moment. Even though the facts were a little muddled, according to their rules I was entitled to the Purple Heart. I snapped the box shut. "I guess I have."

"Better get dressed," Ferraro said as he climbed from his bed. "It's not long before ward rounds. I haven't had time to fix the new shift."

No doubt about Ferraro, he was a wheeler-dealer. I climbed out of bed, found my boots and shirt, then hurriedly dressed. Ferraro explained that he'd organised a jeep to take me back to the Australian hospital. From there it would be a simple matter of catching one of the choppers plying to and fro between Vung Tau and Nui Dat.

I shook hands with everyone, accepting their thanks once more for a great night's entertainment. Ferraro and I walked from the ward as if we were old friends. As we passed the administration office an American nurse looked up at me with a puzzled expression. I smiled at her. She grinned, clasped a hand to her mouth and shook with stifled laughter.

"What's her problem?" I whispered to Ferraro as we hurried past.

"Maybe it's the lipstick stains on your trousers," he grinned.

I glanced down. I was covered with the tell-tale signs of last night's encounter with Li. I whipped off my bush hat and carried it coyly in front of me.

Outside the ward, the bright sun hurt my eyes. The sounds of Vietnam were all around, intruding and urgent. Choppers were throbbing onto the nearby hospital pad, unloading wounded then lifting off to eagerly seek out more. Ambulances streamed to and fro.

An American jeep waited nearby, the driver clutching the wheel and looking impatiently in our direction. Ferraro stopped and tucked his thumbs in his belt. A broad smile creased his face. "Thanks, Aussie." He held out a beefy hand. I gripped it and we stood in silence. The war paused.

I climbed into the jeep beside the driver. Ferraro reached into his trouser pocket and pulled out a thick brown envelope. He tossed it to me. "Open it later," he said as I caught it. He looked over his shoulder towards the ward. "Better get out of here."

The driver snicked the vehicle into gear and we squealed away. We passed through the gate and headed for the Australian hospital. I looked back but Ferraro had gone.

As we drove through the traffic clamouring into Vung Tau, I slit the envelope. It contained four hundred dollars and a "Get well" card signed by eight Americans.

NUI DAT, 0900HRS

Ned Kelly

I watched a landrover pull up outside the orderly room. A trim little Major, wearing neatly pressed summer uniform and a peaked cap with the gleaming justice insignia of the Legal Corps, stepped from the cab. Carrying a briefcase he strode purposefully inside. I heard voices directing him to the Command Post. Just listening to him made me nervous. He represented *the system*, that omnipotent, amorphous green machine which could toss me in jail and throw away the key.

The Major walked into the CP. He was of medium height, slim, with fine features and blonde hair. He wore gold, wire-rimmed spectacles and radiated an aura of self-righteous indignation akin to a virgin medical intern ordered to clap-test brothel workers. I shuddered. He was obviously one of those finicky, pay-attention-to-detail types that I'd always despised. *He* was the real enemy.

"Lieutenant Kelly?" he asked. His voice was soft, reminding me of a snake's hiss.

"Yes, sir," I grunted and slowly stood up. Buggered if I was going to salute him.

"Is there anywhere private where we can talk?" He peered cautiously around the CP. Dave Brown busied himself updating the map. I could see his ears twitching in our direction.

"Outside," I pointed. The Major put his briefcase on a chair and headed for the door. I grabbed my bush hat, buckled on my pistol belt then followed. My hand brushed my pistol as we walked. I realised I could always shoot the little SOB and claim insanity. I'd be back home within twenty-four hours, with polite, concerned doctors asking me about my toilet training. I'd have a neat room with padded walls, clean sheets on a comfortable bed. There'd be cool, fresh milk to drink . . .

We walked towards the knoll overlooking the airfield. The sun burned from an empty blue sky. A Huey hovered impatiently near the refuelling point. It settled in a cloud of dust and the whine of its turbine died.

The Major paused beneath a rubber tree. He removed his cap, tucked it under his left arm and ran his fingers through his hair. Sweat beaded his forehead. "It's hot," he said.

I shrugged. "It's always hot here." I realised he was new to the country. It gave me a smug feeling of superiority. I rested my hands on my hips, my right hand spread above my pistol holster. *Tempting.*

"I've been here five days," the Major continued. 'I'm only staying two weeks. I'll be glad to get back to Australia."

"Two weeks?" I ventured.

"I'm a reserve officer. Legal Corps has the idea that it will broaden our perspective. We all draw two weeks in country, sort of a quick training tour. His expression was almost apologetic. "How long have you been here?"

"Six months," I replied.

The artillery battery fired a quick barrage to the west. The Major flinched then glanced at me.

"Outgoing," I reassured him. I mentally tracked the shells as they arced away into the Thi Vi Hills. I heard the impacts. I hoped someone was dying.

The Major smiled thinly. "I don't know how you put up with the place."

"You get used to it."

"I suppose you can get used to anything," he said as he gazed over the airfield.

"I suppose you do."

He asked suddenly. "How well do you know the Captain?"

The Captain? I figured he meant Queeg. "I don't really know him personally. We talk daily on the phone and I see him when I go to Task Force briefings," I replied. I was in no mood for verbal fencing, particularly from an officer who was only here for a quick ride to gain career Brownie points. "What's this about?" I demanded.

The Major turned and faced me. "Calm down, Lieutenant. You're not in any trouble."

I raised my eyebrows. "But —"

"I know what went on between you and Captain . . . Queeg . . . last night," he said. "Oh, yes, the nickname you gave him is well known around Task Force HQ." He ran his fingers through his hair again. "You didn't think I was here to reprimand you over last night's incident, did you?"

"To be blunt, the system here has its priorities so fucked up I wouldn't be surprised."

He smiled thinly. "Well, I'm not here on a matter of discipline, yours or anyone else's. All I want from you is an outline of the Captain's recent behaviour."

"I don't understand," I said. This sounded encouraging. Maybe Queeg was in the shit. I wondered what he'd done.

"I'll explain fully in a moment. Tell me, have you found his recent behaviour erratic — or unreasonable in any way?"

I looked at the Major suspiciously. He added: "Anything you tell me is off the record."

"He's weird," I began. "Bloody weird."

"Can you elaborate?"

So I told him about Queeg's obsession with written reports, his inflexible work-by-the-book mentality and his impossible to co-operate with nature. Then I outlined last night's events and his fixation about those lost ten minutes. I really socked it to him. It made me feel better.

The Major listened without comment. When I finished he nodded and said: "His demands were unreasonable — his staff confirmed that fact. However, it's unfortunate the man should have acted the way he did. It wasn't normal for him, I assure you."

"It wasn't?"

"Since his arrival here he was experiencing certain . . . domestic difficulties. His wife was seeing another man. Someone had been writing anonymous letters . . ."

I nodded, acutely aware of the letter in my pocket and its importance to me. I'd received good news in yesterday's mail. I could understand Queeg's emotions all too well: the poison-pen letter was a cowardly act towards officers who were under enough pressure as it was.

"Yesterday afternoon he received a letter from his wife telling him she wanted a divorce. Normally, in such circumstances he would have been given emergency leave to go home and try and patch up the situation. But like all mail around here, his letter had been delayed by almost two weeks. It was too late for him to act. So if last night he seemed . . . irrational, then perhaps it was because he was finally tipped over the edge."

"Over the edge?"

"I believe there is a word for it —"

"You mean he went troppo?"

The Major nodded. "Yes. His staff reported that when he came on duty last night he was highly agitated."

So Queeg had flipped. It seemed he was a victim of circumstances. Suddenly I felt sorry for him. The poor bugger must be going through hell. I was surprised I could feel that way about my adversary. No doubt he'd be relieved of duty, then flown back to Australia for a rubber room vacation. I almost envied him.

The Major replaced his cap then looked squarely at me. "Last night, what was the last thing you said to him?"

I hesitated, then replied. "I told him to do us all a favour and go blow his brains out."

The Major nodded. "Well Lieutenant, after his phone call to you, the Captain went to his tent and put a pistol to his head."

*Nowhere to run,
nowhere to hide . . .*

Ned Kelly

I felt a cold, hollow feeling in the pit of my stomach as I watched the Major climb into his landrover and drive away. I walked slowly back into the CP. Dave Brown looked up from his magazine with raised eyebrows. I ignored him. He sensed my mood and continued reading. His transistor radio was playing softly in the background: *Galveston, Oh Galveston . . .*

The artillery battery south of the field thumped six rounds away. Something in the back of my mind told me the shells were falling close into the north-east. I didn't care.

Ross Hutchinson was at the wall map, briefing Mike Dawson before his first flight around the Province. I went to the calendar where Dave kept tag of everyone's time in country. I counted the days again, reassuring myself that I was on the downhill run. I had one hundred and eighty-two days left. I could take heart that before long I'd be back home and could forget about this asylum.

I saw that a day had been struck off against Mike's name. I looked at him and he smiled. "At least now I've only three hundred and sixty-four days to go," he said.

"And I've just passed the halfway mark," I replied. The comparison cheered me.

Hutch turned from the map. "I've got bad news for both of you," he said as he slung his M-16 over his shoulder and headed for the door.

"What bad news?" I called to him.

Hutch paused. "This year's a Leap Year." He looked at

Mike and grinned. "No bastard's got three hundred and sixty-five days to go!"

Mike's jaw dropped. He shook his head then looked pleadingly at me. I checked the calendar. 1968 was a leap year but the calendar didn't make allowances for February the twenty-ninth. Mike still had three hundred and sixty-five days to go. I would pass the halfway mark tomorrow!

I walked to the bench, picked up the chrome microphone and screamed: *"Fuck Vee-et-nam!"*

ONE DAY AT A TIME

D.J. Dennis was born in 1945 in Manly, Sydney. A keen surfer, he spent much of his youth skipping classes from school to put in an hour's surfing. After leaving school he studied electrical engineering at the University of New South Wales, but left to become an advertising copywriter for a national food company. He was also a competitive swimmer, achieving placings in state and Australian championships and trying out in 1964 for the Tokyo Olympics. When conscription was announced in 1964, Dennis left his job and spent the next eight months surfing between Sydney and Brisbane. After his number came up in the conscription lottery, he was selected for officers' training school and, on graduating, was posted to the Army's 16 Light Aircraft Squadron in Queensland as assistant operations officer. In August 1967 he was sent to Vietnam as 161 Reconaissance Flight's operations officer. After the war, he was promoted to Captain and spent two years training with the Airforce and Department of Civil Aviation in control towers and schools around Australia. For the next three years he served as the Aviation Corps Senior Air Traffic Officer at the Army's airbase at Oakey, Queensland. At age twenty-nine, Dennis returned to civilian life. He has since become involved in the Agent Orange debate and has managed companies in Indonesia and Australia. In 1982 he formed his own software company and now spends his time managing the company and writing.